I AM

My True Self

Let Go,
Feel Free,
and Awaken Your Dream Life

DARLA LUZ

Cover design by MiblArt

Interior formatting by Jen Henderson at Wild Words Formatting

Landing page design by Mahal Montes

Although the author has made every effort to ensure that the information in this book was correct at press time, the author and publisher do not assume and hereby disclaim any liability to any party for any loss, damage, or disruption caused by errors or omissions, whether such errors or omissions result from negligence, accident, or any other cause.

The resources in this book are provided for informational purposes only and should not be used to replace the specialized training and professional judgment of a health care or mental health care professional. Neither the author nor the publisher can be held responsible for the use of the information provided within this book. Please always consult a trained professional before making any decision regarding treatment of yourself or others.

I AM My True Self: Let Go, Feel Free, and Awaken Your Dream Life—1st edition

ISBN: 978-1-7348913-2-4

BOOKS BY DARLA LUZ

HEART SERIES

The Heart of Attention
Free yourself from stress, and all inner conflict
for good creating a heart-felt life of perfection

I AM My True Self
Let go, Feel Free, and awaken your dream life

*Consciousness is as simple as looking into
the face of a flower and realizing a shared connection.
We too open to the light in strength and beauty.*

—*Darla Luz*

DEDICATION

To you the reader

You are much more connected than you know to the beauty and perfection of an infinite universe. May your light shine ever so brilliantly as you connect more deeply to an effortless, unlimited universal flow showing up in every corner of your life!

To my husband Danny for the endless support and enthusiasm for my life's work. I feel fortunate to have grown with you because we now understand the true meaning of love.

To my editor, Brian for his tireless attention to maintain the detail of clarity. Thank you for offering suggestions on wording while placing a priority on preserving my "authentic voice."

FREE MINIBOOK

To accelerate your path of letting go, feeling free, and awakening, it is important to connect *in peaceful awareness* with your true self.

This handy **free** minibook will make it easy to connect with your true self as you go about your day because every connection from the book, **I AM My True Self** is here. Whether you keep it next to your bedside or on your desktop, each connection will only take a few seconds of your time!

Remember that you are taking a quantum leap as you let go of daily stresses, anxieties, and past sadness to improve your situations, circumstances, and relationships!

You will receive the minibook in your email. Please check spam if you do not see it.

Name _____ Email _____

Visit
www.Darlaluzbooks.com/hoaworkbook
for your free minibook

TABLE OF CONTENTS

EDITOR'S PREFACE

I am grateful for Darla Luz's wisdom. When I reached the lowest low in my life, when my mental pain became physical—my body and mind collapsing under the weight of a world of stress that held me down—Darla Luz saved me with her wisdom.

It was my son's birthday and just the day before I had suffered a final loss of thousands of dollars that doomed my new business venture. I had risked everything, including my retirement, over the previous 3 years.

But today I needed to put that out of mind.

On our way to the party, I was pulled over by a police officer. He had noticed my expired license plate tags. I pleaded with him that it was my son's birthday. But he made the inconvenient decision to impound my car for fees that had gone unpaid, while I was desperately trying to extend the life of my business.

Embarrassed in front of my children, I carefully unloaded the car and we walked a mile with my son's gifts to the nearest place of business. I pleaded by phone with my ex-wife to meet us an hour away and to let me borrow her car. I put on the best face I could and I turned this situation into a game for my kids.

Finally, on our way again, while driving on the freeway in my ex-wife's van, I felt a sudden pang in my chest while passing an 18-wheeler. It was a piercing feeling of fear and anxiety, one which I had never felt before in my life.

Suddenly this routine event, passing a big rig on the freeway, left me in a panicked state. With my whole world collapsing in on itself, I almost couldn't move yet I managed to drive off the freeway to safety. In the confusion, I soon realized that I should seek advice from Darla Luz.

I cautiously got back on the freeway as she guided me on my journey with her soothing voice and crystal-clear wisdom. Darla told me to picture myself as an observer of the situation from far away. She instructed me to observe with objectivity how my brain was working in a cycle of worry and anxiety— to focus on observing that fact.

I immediately began to calm down as I was better able to rationalize and understand what was happening. Without hesitation and with an ethereal calmness, she proceeded to do what no therapist had been able to do. She shifted my understanding of the world—of how I could view a seeming crisis. She continued to guide me for the duration of the hour-long trip. On that day, I became a true believer in her rare abilities to heal.

THE ANCIENTS, THE NEW AGE AND DARLA LUZ

In The Dhammapada, a collection of the Buddha's words, we are told that, "Our life is shaped by our mind; we become what we think. Joy follows a pure thought like a shadow that never leaves." Written over 2,000 years ago and reflecting an ancient wisdom, this line could be from one of Darla Luz's books.

Her writing is clear and speaks to the reader in easy-to-understand language. She has a way of distilling what is important in a philosophy and getting the message out clearly to those of us who desperately need it.

In a famous interview Oprah asked "how do we get to the True Self?" It's a relevant question and millions of people want to know the answer. And here in this book, Darla Luz shows you the way.

"The Self is the light reflected by all." Echoing these words from the Bhagavad Gita, Darla will explain here in this book how to find your true Self. And she will show you how to access the power of this light.

Darla Luz reminds us in this book that "you have already done more than you know." You are ready now to begin the journey on your path of awakening and she will help you take your first few steps.

Luz tells us that "setting an intention to the truth in all areas of your life is an expansion on the path of awakening."

Without further ado, it is now time to begin your journey with Darla and "revel in the peaceful depth of infinity." Enjoy!

Brian Montes

INTRODUCTION

A most beautiful truth that exists in the world today is the beauty and perfection that is within you, within each and every one of us. It is infinite, it is without limits, and it is powerful; has always been there, and will always be there. And, it is within you now in this moment. Another most beautiful truth is that whatever you are feeling, whether a worry, an uncertainty, or anything zapping your energy and bringing you down, is unimportant and powerless! And since it is powerless, and yes, weak, the power within you can easily dissolve it.

You might be wondering how such beauty and perfection could exist in a world filled with uncertainty, strife, and seemingly endless problems.

One of the most important things we can learn in the world today is who we are. To learn the capacity each of us has, not only to create our very best life, but to discover our capacity to help a world that is desperately in need of the power within each of us.

This capacity is always available and easily accessible. Imagine you as an infant, taking your first steps, carefully, without anxiety and without stress. There was something inherent within you that seemed to guide you, as if propelling you on toward the finish line, helping you master just the right harmony and balance; the perfection needed to achieve a most important goal in your life so that you could flourish and evolve.

Perfection and beauty continued in the words that rolled off your tongue, in the miracle of hands that could grasp and hold, and in the motor skills that took care of your every move.

Beauty and perfection appeared, again, in your glowing skin and sparkling eyes, and in a demeanor that was open, real, and genuine so that you could be nurtured, nourished, protected, cherished, and loved.

In the moments when you were learning and discovering, you were undaunted and carefree, fascinated by a world that surrounded you, filled to the brim with a spectrum of colors and textures everywhere you looked.

You believed in the wondrous magic of life. You loved the sound of crackling leaves in autumn, the feel of moist grass in summer, the glistening snow in winter, and the scent of flowers in spring. Gleefully running, jumping, somersaulting, and climbing trees, your only worry was that Santa would find out that you had been "naughty" and not "nice."

All too soon something changed within. Difficulties and uncertainties took their toll in the ever-changing landscape of your life. You became like a tree whose tense and rigid limbs broke easily in stormy weather; your vitality, energy, and vigor swept away by torrential rains.

It does not matter how long you have felt the difficulty and uncertainty of life that we all have experienced. The carefree enthusiasm and aliveness that so many had as a child, we can get back. Even if you do not remember ever having it, you too, can start living the same magical fresh wonder and awe of life, because it is available to each and every one of us in this very moment no matter our age, no matter where we come from!

You will discover here that every sadness, disillusionment, tension, or worry is false! The truth of life is joy, aliveness, and bliss!

Within the pages of this book, you will reach and discover the magnificent and immense energy within you that will put you on the path to an awakened, magical life. And it is all about breathing and being who you truly are... your genuine, real, true Self!

Are you ready to create your best life?

Chapter One

BEING TRUTH IN PRESENCE AND AWARENESS

The way we come into this world is a hint on how our life is meant to be lived.

You came into this world through your breath, bestowing you with aliveness and well-being. You were present and aware in the moment, with focused attention on the warmth, nourishment, and nurturing touch. This pure, clear moment could not be diminished by a past or future.

The way we come into this world is a hint on how our life is meant to be lived.

As you grew from infancy, you continued living in pure presence. If something startled you, and in the next moment something made you laugh you could easily forget being startled. In an instant, your resilient nature could let go.

A SHIFT IN AWARENESS
IS HOW WE LET GO

Letting go of all inner conflict is the only way we can get back the wondrous joy and awe that we deserve.

Today, it seems, we live increasingly distracted, holding on, stuck, and trapped in *focused awareness* of the dilemmas and complexities of an outer world, unable to let go. We are more often than not blinded to the beauty and perfection of life all around us, which you will learn within these pages can be tapped into to help us live an easier life of less struggle.

Where, in this moment, are you holding your awareness?

Are your thoughts in the past? Whenever our thoughts and emotions are in the past, eighty per cent, or more, of these thoughts are useless, circling, go-nowhere thoughts of sadness, disillusionment, anger, resentment, regret; endless inner-conflict that may continue for hours, weeks, and sometimes years! If our thoughts are in the future, they often result in worry, a fantasy and illusion of something that *might* happen in the future.

It is important to remember that where we hold our attention will grow in our experience, and reflect back situations and circumstances that seem to just happen to us. You will be reminded in this book, again and again, that **where you hold your attention grows in your experience**! Another way of saying this is, "What you think about, you become." If you keep thinking depressive thoughts, you will experience depression. So that the more focus and attention you put on any situation in life, how you *feel* will either worsen or make you feel better, depending on your perspective of it. This, taps into Universal Laws that have been around for eternity and are stable, unwavering, solid, and real.

REALIZING WHO YOU ARE BEYOND THE EGO CHANGES YOUR LIFE

You might be wondering: Just *how* do I "go beyond" my personality self, the false ego self, so that I can change my life for the better?

In each of the practices and connections in between these pages, you will hold your attention and awareness in peaceful relaxation *now*, in this moment. In the same moment you feel peaceful, *you have let go* of all inner conflict of the ego that has caused you to suffer! You are, in the moment you let go, gently lifted out of the stories, memories, beliefs, feelings, and emotions that have kept you stuck and held you back from creating your best life. Feeling your Self in pure, peaceful awareness and letting go of inner conflict is how you "go beyond" the false ego, its false narratives, memories, thoughts, and emotions.

Letting go of all that causes hardship in life is not a thought coming from your everyday, ordinary mind, telling you that you "should" let go, it comes about from a *feeling* of peace and awareness.

And the more often you experience an inward journey with a feeling of peaceful awareness, the more you will realize your true-identity and true Self, a deeper sense of your presence. And this will happen without effort, without hard work.

Knowing who you are—a peaceful, aware true Self—will transform your life, help you to awaken, and take you on a path of Self-Realization and Enlightenment.

As you practice and connect to who you truly are, you are tapping into the *infinite invisible energies* that exist all around and within each and every one of us. These are the energies that are tapped into as we learn to ride a bike, swim, dance, sing, or play a musical instrument. The more we practice, the more effortless flow we create. And the more joy, exhilaration, and vitality these effortless energies bring to our lives.

In fact, all creative pursuits tap into this infinite invisible energy that creates beauty and perfection in the world.

Why *couldn't your* life, every corner of it, fill with beauty and perfection?

In this book, you will become aware of the magnificence within you the more you practice *being* your true Self.

As you progress in your practice, you will naturally, without effort, realize you are not just the ordinary, everyday mind and emotions of lesser energies that produces hardship in life, nor are you just your physical body that will end with this physical existence. You are an eternal, infinite being, very much connected to the infinite invisible energies of perfection and beauty!

Realizing who you are will help you let go of the commotion in your head; the unwanted stories, memories, and thoughts, so that you no longer suffer emotions that weigh you down. In discovering the truth of who you are—your true Self and identity—your life changes because you open to a higher world, a higher dimension, or, if you would rather think of it as a *powerful energy*, that is fine too!

This vast power opens door after door to opportunities, solutions, and the energy and vitality to move your life forward.

This infinite, invisible, but very real world, beyond our third-dimensional earth plane life, is pure light. Light is an invisible energy that you will use as you imagine, picture, see, and feel it to create your best life. More will be said about the energy of light in following chapters.

If you are feeling stuck in endless thoughts and emotions that dampen any hope for a better future. If you wake up dreading another day, with increasing worries and concerns. Or, even if you occasionally have thoughts of worry that seem to loop endlessly, suppressing your vitality and enthusiasm for life, you may want to open and understand a new way of being in the world.

There is no need for you to experience a problem or a challenge that causes hardship and suffering. You can open now, in this very moment and awaken to a new reality, a new way of being, letting go effortlessly of the inner conflict of stress, fear, sadness; all inner conflicts and concerns of a difficult world.

The core and center of every spiritual teaching is goodness and purity and it is reached either in the silent, surrendering energies of prayer, meditation, or contemplation.

You are reaching the core heart of yourself in silent, peaceful, awareness in this book and allowing pure goodness into your life, changing your life in miraculously magical ways.

You may replace what is being called, and I am calling the true Self here as either Divine Self, higher Self, Spirit, Soul, or simply energy.

You may think of your true Self as your Spirit in Christ, your Spirit in Buddha, or simply the energy within. As you practice and connect, you may call upon Jesus Christ, your guide, or your guardian angel for assistance to help you transcend the ordinary false self.

It does not matter whether we are spiritual or not. Each of us has a birthright to an incredible and true energy within, and is available now to begin transforming every aspect of our life in unimaginable, beautiful ways despite our background and what we believe.

Every feeling of sadness and discontent, of feeling stuck and trapped in endless thoughts that tell you of the lack and limitations in your life, can be removed and vanished for good, replaced by a new enthusiasm and vitality for life.

We will call these feelings of sadness and discontent the false ego identity. Most of humanity believes their identity, who they are, is the false ego of "naturally occurring" problems and inner conflict. Most of humanity believes that the suffering that this false identity brings into life is normal! More will be said about the false ego self in a following chapter.

Please open your mind! You are about to open door after door of what will seem like magic into your life!

There is nothing to lose and everything to gain as you practice and connect to your true Self and identity, your Greater Self. You are experiencing higher levels of mind. As you relax, the only side-effect will be an experience of calm inner peace, a sense of freedom, and a letting go.

The more relaxed and calm you feel, the easier it is to reach and explore your innermost essence, the real and true you; eventually expressing and embodying inner peace and awareness in daily life.

WHAT YOU WILL GET
OUT OF THIS BOOK

- When you are aware of your breath in the moment, the false ego self of unwanted thoughts and emotions simply vanishes. You are free in that moment. There is no struggle, no trying hard to do anything.

- As you hold awareness and live as your true Self, your true identity, moment to moment, you are no longer blocked by useless thoughts of lack and limitation that have held you back, sabotaging your goals and dreams.

- You will discover an amazingly simple method that can dissolve, change, and transform problematic situations in your life.

- You will discover how to let go and turn away quickly and easily from lesser energies that bring you down.

- Before you know it, one day you will notice your life is more peaceful, and situations that once bothered you are no longer there.

- You will experience a vast and unlimited true Self that can effortlessly create abundance in every area of your life.

MY STORY

I began a spiritual path in 2011 that gave me a new sense of direction. Before that, I was an emotional wreck. I worried all the time about things that never came to pass, and thought that I was my past, with its ups and downs, regrets, doubts, and grievances. Everything I tried was an uphill battle that I thought I had to work hard for and conquer to have a successful life, and it was usually a monetary goal; never something of more significance and meaning. And the goals that I did accomplish never gave me a sense of fulfillment or true joy.

I indulged in stories of past hurtful scenarios that I thought came from others, never realizing that they came from my own perspective, my own point of view. Even as I began my spiritual path, I did not have a handle on relentless thoughts and emotions that blocked a true enjoyment of life.

Fortunately, my spiritual path led me to my purpose, the writing of my first book, "The Heart of Attention," and now a second! If someone had told me I was going to write a book, I would have never believed it.

The "Heart of Attention" is the first book of this series, The Heart Series. However, if you are reading this book first, you are still benefitting from experiencing your true Self, a most important thing to do in life.

The major life-changes I have experienced, just in the last year and a half as I wrote this book, have come from the practices and connections to my true Self that you are about to experience here.

Because I practice being my true Self as often as I can, moment to moment, throughout my day, I feel the vitality, energy, joy, reassurance, and comfort that, in a spirit of surrender, my life is flowing in harmony with my highest future. I feel more abundance in every area. I am getting more done, have better health, a greater ability to resist that which does not move my life forward. I wake up each morning with the realization that we can, indeed, create a life of our dreams. And that includes everyone.

As you practice and connect to your true Self and identity here, I guarantee that you *will* experience inner peace and less struggle in your life!

However, *maintaining an on-going and consistent connection to your true Self* as you go about your day will open many more amazing gifts in life! Your new-found *awareness* is what will help you take note of even the most trivial gift that makes its way into your life!

The practices and connections that you are about to experience in this book have been inspired mostly by the research and study I have done of Consciousness and the true Self. This book has also been created from the knowing coming from the higher Consciousness of my true Self, as well as the assistance I have asked for and the guidance I have been given. In a state of euphoria that each of us can experience in a higher level of Consciousness, which you are about to practice here, I have paused to give light (energy) to each practice and connection.

The practices and connections will become familiar enough to do in just seconds. Practice and do the connections in their order.

Then, as you become familiar with them, pick and choose each practice or connection that feels comfortable and speaks to you, always keeping in mind that a connection with your true identity and true Self is one of the most important things you can do.

Remember to stay on track! It may take weeks or months to experience the gifts that *will* come your way as you keep practicing and keep the connection going!

I want all the good that can flow into life, all the gifts, and realizations that can be gotten here to include everyone.

Many people today are distracted by the dilemmas of an outer world, which is not the path and creation of their best life. We, each of us, were born with a birthright to an inner magnificence that has always been there, and will always be there to support and create our best life, even the life of our dreams!

All that has weighed you down and made you suffer is false. The false ego pretending to be you will be exposed and dissolved into nothingness as you practice and connect here. As you shine your light (energy), exposing the false ego, you will see clearly what has made you suffer.

Another most beautiful and important truth is that the spiritual path of awakening into Self-Realization and enlightenment opens for us a path to help others. With a more illuminated light, your mere presence will help a world in jeopardy. The path that you are embarking on in the pages of this book, will take you to that expanded, more luminous light. It is a path to be a very much needed light in the world!

Chapter Two

THE PRESENT MOMENT

The realization of a deeper sense of Presence, your true Self

Would you believe that the answer to every problem, every worry, exists in the center and core of your being, your source, the source of all life, the universe within you; an indestructible, immeasurable, *true Self*?

Your true Self allows a more effortless and easier way of life. There is no need to force a realization of your true-identity. You will know who you are as you experience calming peace and awareness. Going beyond the ordinary, false ego mind and false self is simply relaxing in peaceful awareness.

We do not have to live with difficulty. We can live a life that is better; more graceful, effortless, and unproblematic. We reach our true Self through "getting out of our heads" and into a peaceful, calm state.

When your attention is on peace and awareness, as you practice and connect in this book, sadness and worry do not enter your mind. In fact, any lesser energy that harms *cannot* enter your mind.

TRUTH IS NOW

What could be truer than an aware peacefulness with every breath you take in this moment? You are in the simple and pure state of *the present moment*, aware and at peace with all that surrounds you.

In the following practice, you are *being* your real and true Self.

PRACTICE #1

BEING A DEEPER SENSE OF YOUR PRESENCE, YOUR TRUE SELF

1. Put focused awareness on your breath as you inhale. Exhale out all concerns and worries of an outer world. Continue inhaling and exhaling comfortably in the same way, putting awareness on the center of your being, the *you* within.

2. Relax your neck, jaw, head, the muscles around your eyes. Relax any tension in your chest, stomach, your arms, and hands. Continue relaxing your thighs, legs, and feet. Feel the increased awareness. You are more present in this moment. You are more aware of the sounds and scents in the room, the feeling of your clothes on the surface of your body. More aware of a feeling of peace moving through you.

3. Use your increased awareness to make yourself more comfortable; relaxing the muscles throughout your body even more.

4. Can you feel a deeper relaxation, and more and more peace? This deeper sense of peace is leading you to a deeper sense of your presence—your true Self.

5. You are *letting go* and awakening to the real and true you, and have taken the first steps on the path of Self-Realization.

You have done more than you know. By going inward and experiencing your true Self, you are awakening a realization of who you truly are.

Awareness and peacefulness will assist you in realizing that you are more than just your body, emotions, and thoughts. You have, in the moment you are aware and at peace, let go of thoughts and emotions that cause hardship and suffering. Through peaceful awareness, you are discovering how to turn away quickly and easily from destructive lesser energies that no longer serve you.

As you practice and connect in the following chapters, you will discover there are more ways to turn away from *lesser energies* that harm you emotionally and physically. Keeping your awareness in *higher energies* moment to moment is what you are aspiring to do here so that you can stay in the higher vibrations that reflect higher, better outcomes in your life.

Little by little, you are releasing and letting go of the trivial situations and problems that once loomed large in your focus and attention. More and more, you open to endless gifts from your true Self like awareness, harmony, inner peace, and guidance. There are many more gifts it gladly and genuinely wants to give you as you are ready, open, and receptive.

Even if, at first, as you do practice #1, you can have awareness on only your breath, it is a good start. Practice makes perfect! Please do not be hard on yourself. With practice, you will sense or feel a deeper you. Because your true Self exists beyond the mind of thoughts, you may not think you have connected. However, this Self is a conscious energy that is aware of you in every moment and welcomes your growing recognition of it!

Maintaining a connection with your true Self is simple, but it is not easy, especially, in a world of distractions and a bombardment of information. Add to this the energies of negativity that fill our environment with chaos-ridden thoughts and emotions coming from lesser energies that are taken in as our own. They are impersonal and false energies, and they block us from knowing our true-identity and true Self.

RECREATING INNER PEACE

Can you feel the deepest, most profound inner peace you have ever felt? Remember that when you are in a state of peace, the lesser energies that weigh down and depress are not evident. You do not feel fear, anger, remorse, regret, resentment; there is forgiveness of yourself and everyone when you have inner peace in this moment! And the more profound your aware, inner peace, the better.

You can recreate peace by remembering what inner peace feels like. Get good at it! Most likely, you have a good memory of a vacation because it is in those moments that we feel light-hearted and free. For the most part, when we have a memory of something that felt joyful, there is a lightness that is free from inner turmoil. We can take from a memory of a moment in life that gives us a high energetic feeling. We grow when we learn to recreate the feeling of inner peace because our attention is focused on energies of a higher vibration and frequency, which attracts only good into life.

The simple act of choosing to feel inner peace puts us on a higher level of Consciousness that is aligned and attracts the energies of magical gifts that make their appearance, manifesting in our reality; a most important thing to do in life. As you practice here, learn the feeling of inner peace, then recreate it as often as you can throughout your day.

As you do the practices and connections here, let go of an image or a feeling of your physical body. Simply learn to feel as if you are formless and shapeless. The idea is to be so peacefully aware that you feel as if you are floating or flying. You may not experience it in the beginning, however, with practice you will.

For thirty minutes a day I looked out at a peaceful lake view that I wrote about in the first book of this series, the "Heart of Attention." For months, and for just thirty minutes per day, I enjoyed, in serene stillness, the effortless way I was able to release troublesome thoughts and emotions by simply focusing in non-thought, as best as I could, on the currents on the lake. Even though I did not yet have the tools I am giving you here, it was from this clear, peaceful, and pure state of awareness that I received an answer to my problem that proved to be perfect. Amazingly, I never asked for an answer to my challenge, it simply came to me through my daily engagement in silent, peaceful awareness. In following chapters, you will discover how to get answers to situations in your life. And it all begins with peaceful awareness!

Chapter Three

WHO AM I?

*Knowing who you truly are changes
your life in unimaginable ways*

What if you knew for a fact that all you needed to let go of all the chaos and uncertainty of a difficult world was within you?

That letting go is as simple as taking a conscious, aware, peaceful breath. Because in the same moment you take a deep, relaxing breath, you shift your attention. And all that has caused hardship and suffering in daily life vanishes into nothingness!

Would you be willing to *commit* to knowing who you truly are if you knew that you could transform relationships, abundance, energy, and love?

That if you committed to an intention of a shift in focused awareness of your centered, alive, breathing Self, you would in weeks and months transform every corner of your life!

Would you *intend* a commitment of ten to twenty second connections several times a day knowing that the doors to opportunities, potentials, and possibilities would open-up in your life?

And would you be willing to intend and commit to knowing who you truly are because it is one of the most important steps you can take in life?

Are you ready to commit to your true Self and its gifts of qualities of Consciousness?

A commitment is something you do to fulfill a deep desire— an intention. It is the "doing" part of the intention—the accomplishment of a goal. Commitment is what drives us to go to a job or to school each morning. It is what motivates us to follow through and do those important things, day in and day out.

You can commit to claim your true Self as who you are by following through and committing to do the practices and connections here. As you do, you activate an infinite number of gifts, including transforming your life, infusing new Consciousness, awareness, and understandings, as well as many more gifts that are beyond measure.

In the following connection, find the words that will help you commit to knowing your true-identity.

Connection in Seconds:

INTENDING A COMMITMENT TO KNOWING YOUR TRUE IDENTITY—YOUR TRUE SELF

Take several comfortable breaths and feel inner peace spreading throughout your body. Let go of any unwanted thoughts and emotions of the past and future, simply *Being* yourself, peacefully and aware in this moment. You may imagine energy all around you. Or you may imagine Divine beings of light or a Divine being of your choice asking if you would like to make a commitment to know your true identity, your true Self. You may affirm, "I commit to knowing my true Self," "I am my true Self," "I claim my true Self as who I am," or by simply using the words that feel meaningful and comfortable as you say them. In the moment you commit, you are taking a new direction in your life. Many things will change for the better.

As you practice and connect to a higher Consciousness within these pages, you are in the vast, infinite, and abundant space (spaciousness) you see as you look out at a vast and infinite night sky. You are a miniature version of this Universal limitless boundlessness which can be brought into your life.

As you sustain higher Consciousness you awaken to who you truly are. You gain confidence as you realize that you, and you alone, are the authority of your life. You now realize you have within you the answers and solutions to all situations you experience, helping you to feel reassured and more at peace with life.

As you practice and connect, you are discovering how to steer clear of lesser energies of worries, anxieties, and stressful situations that have held you back, not allowing the higher energies that come from a higher Consciousness of joy, inner peace, and self-love to make their appearance in your life.

Your true Self of this higher Consciousness clears the way, helping you to create a life that is no longer ordinary. As you simply intend to connect to your true-Self and identity, and relax and open in awareness and peace, new understandings, wisdom, energy, answers, solutions, and qualities of Consciousness come from beyond the ordinary mind.

The following connection will help you understand the unconditional, loving energy that is always available to give you the inner guidance that can help create your best life.

This is a connection you can do in ten to twenty seconds, once you become familiar with it.

Connection in Seconds:

DEEPENING A CONNECTION TO YOUR TRUE SELF

In silence, intend a connection to your true Self and relax your entire body into the most peacefully aware you can feel. As you do, you are contacting and opening to your true Self.

You are, in this moment, open to receive its guidance, answers, solutions, inspiration and much, much more that your true Self is willing and able to offer you. Put aware focus on your breath, a comfortable inhaling and exhaling so that you can quiet your mind and let go of thinking, even if just for a moment. Put peaceful awareness on the center of your body and imagine that you are looking out through your eyes as your true Self of beautiful perfection. Allow this Self to draw and magnetize you into itself. Feel the peaceful stillness. To connect more deeply, you may release any beliefs that tell you that you are separate from your true Self, that block you from contacting your true Self and receiving the gifts it eagerly wants to give you. In peaceful awareness you may ask for answers, solutions, transformation, qualities of inner peace, joy, and loving kindness or simply rest in silent non-thought because your true Self knows, more than you, exactly what you need.

You gain a deeper connection as you stop often, in just seconds, during your day to consciously acknowledge your true Self. A connection in moments of several seconds a few times a day increases awareness and a realization of who you truly are!

It is important to remember that you need to intend a connection, relax, and open to receive answers, solutions, and gifts of Consciousness from your true Self.

Remember that it is okay if you prefer to think of your true Self as your Spirit in Christ or your Spirit in Buddha. Or you may think of your true Self as simply energy. In a few practices and connections throughout this book you may be asked to call upon a Divine Being to help bring about the beauty of your innermost Self. Whether you call upon Jesus Christ, your guide, or your guardian angel, your call is heard instantly because there is no time and no space in the higher dimensions.

Most important is the awareness of the vast, infinite energy each of us has within to overcome the suffering that comes from a difficult, divided world.

In the moment you intend a connection and relax, you *are* open to receive the gifts that this inner Self is offering in every moment. *An intention is a focused, one-pointed, decision you make.*

When you commit and intend to reach your true Self, you set in motion changes and new directions. As you intend and open in a relaxed, peaceful, aware state, you are allowing and inviting the light and higher Consciousness of your true Self into your life, accelerating your growth.

As you look out through your eyes as your true Self of infinite intelligence, all-knowing wisdom, and unconditional love, each time you make a connection you are also practicing an expression of those qualities in your daily life.

This is the true Self within that is free of lesser energies that cause harm. There is no judgment, no anger, no unforgiveness in the higher levels of Consciousness of your true Self. In essence, you are practicing higher levels of *Being.*

Silence is a powerful way to connect with your true Self. In silence, your true Self is more able to infuse you with its qualities of Consciousness like inner peace, wisdom, and loving kindness. This is because your mind is clearer and freer of lesser energies like anxiety, stress, and sadness. You awaken much more than you know as you are present in peaceful silence. You are experiencing, in aware silent *presence,* the energy of light of your formless, powerful, true Self. More will be said about the energy of light in following chapters.

The silence experienced in prayer, meditation, or contemplation is a powerful energy that is experienced beyond the ordinary mind. Because of this, you may not think you have connected. However, whenever you have an intention to connect and a sincere openness to receive, *know* that you *have* connected!

RESTING IN NON-THOUGHT

Can you rest in silent non-thought? Feeling at peace in non-thought brings you the spaciousness needed to receive the insights, answers, and inspirational ideas. Silent non-thought is powerful because the non-sensical commotion coming from the false self is no longer there, and the energies of goodness from your true Self can now make their way into your mind—and life! In silence, there is nothing you need to do, and you still receive unimaginable good flowing through every corner of your life!

As you progress in the practices and connections here, it will become easier for you to simply rest in non-thought.

REMOVING LIMITING, UNWANTED THOUGHTS

Consider unwanted thoughts that get in the way and stop you from creating your best life—the limiting beliefs and opinions that block you from knowing who you truly are.

It is important to remove any beliefs or thoughts that may hinder reaching and receiving gifts from this higher, true Self that is omnipotent, omnipresent, and omniscient. This is the energy within you that is infinite power, everywhere at once, and all-knowing wisdom.

Are there thoughts that tell you that it is not possible to dissolve the thoughts and emotions that are the cause of distress and suffering? Do you have a belief that problems are a normal part of life? Is there a belief you may have that you are a separate identity, the "you" with a past of sad stories and memories?

Any thought that tells you it is too difficult to practice living your true, genuine, and real Self is a thought that stops you from creating your best life! Take a few moments to consider your thoughts. Remember not to get involved nor indulge in limiting thoughts and emotions because they are false. You are a limitless being who can create your best life through your true Self, your true Spirit. As you continue your practice here, you are discovering many ways that can easily dissolve these unwanted thoughts!

ASKING FOR SOMETHING SPECIFIC OR RESTING IN NON-THOUGHT

As you feel a deepening connection, you may ask for unlimited abundance, improved relationships, solutions, or answers. You may ask for your true Self's qualities of Consciousness so that you can express them in an outer world. Or you may simply rest in non-thought.

Whether you ask for something specific or rest in non-thought, always acknowledge the good that comes back to you.

Notice if you have any answers or solutions after a deeper connection to your true Self. You may have a deep peaceful feeling, a deeper breath, an insight, an impulse, a behavior, a thought that seems perfect. An answer may come with profound awareness or something you just "know."

You may hear words from a soft voice that is a perfect solution to a situation. It may be a message you receive—like a thought that comes to you seemingly from "out of nowhere." It may come in a dream, something random you read, or it may come to you in a "knowing" way that is perfect.

Even if you do not notice anything, you have made a connection. And an answer or a solution, a blessing, or a gift, may show up in an instant. Or it may come to you days or weeks later.

In the first book of this series, "The Heart of Attention," I wrote about an inspired idea I received by being "pulled" to a destination in an aware, alert, peacefulness. And it proved to be a perfect idea that saved my family from homelessness! Unbelievably, I never asked for a solution. I simply rested in non-thought as I contemplated a beautiful lake. This shows how the Divine Spirit within knows exactly what we need to move our life forward.

As you continue intending to connect to your true Self, you will soon feel or know when connection is made. You may sense its energy or simply know you have connected through a deeper breath, or a feeling that all is well. You may feel a lightness—an opening of your heart center. In whatever way you connect as you begin these practices and connections, your true Self is always available, ready to offer you the best life it truly wants to give you. Even if you do not have a sense of your true Self, much is still occurring within.

Remember to do this connection often and not become impatient and wonder when you will receive insight, inspiration, or a solution to a situation. The more often you connect, surrender and trust, the better the connection, and the more open you become to receive.

In following practices and connections in this book, you will explore and ultimately express and live your true Self—the Greater Self within yourself.

I usually connect in restful non-thought and life seems to flow in balance and harmony. I am at the right place at the right time in which events seem to fall into place effortlessly. I have noticed that through an impulse, I get up to do something. And I realize later that the impulse and behavior was the perfect thing to do to help me move forward in the accomplishment of a goal.

As you become your true Self, manifesting and creating becomes easier than trying to bring about your dreams and aspirations through the ordinary, everyday mind—the false ego identity. Living your true Self allows the Universal flow to flood through your life, making it better, more flowing, and harmonious, as you explore, become, and express your true Self.

The true Self is an aware, alive, Consciousness that knows you intimately—your past, your present, and your future—and wants to give you the best you are open to receive. It has unconditional love for you, and communes with an infinite, unlimited universe, bringing back into your life infinite unlimited good in every area of life.

Door after door opens to transformation, solutions, opportunities, answers, improved relationships, and to claiming the higher qualities of this Self of a higher Consciousness as your own.

As you connect, you are bringing back into your life a new way of being, thinking, relating, and living.

Chapter Four

BEING YOUR TRUE SELF

*Maintaining a connection to your Source, your true
Self is the key to the creation of your best life*

There has been a significant expansion of Consciousness in
the world today. Humanity may not have a true
understanding of the great news this growth and evolvement
of our awareness represents.

Did you know that when you are aware, you *are* in
Consciousness? Awareness *is* Consciousness; a very pure,
unpolluted, clean, and wholesome state that heals life.

When we put attention on the stories, narratives, and
memories of past sadness or worry of the future, that is what
grows in our experience, manifesting as situations, events, and
circumstances in life. Whether we believe it or not, our
thoughts and emotions create our reality.

A focused awareness and attention of our surroundings in this moment allows us to *let go* of the lesser energies that create havoc in our lives. In the same moment we are aware of our Self within or of our surroundings, we have let go of anger, sadness, disillusionment, unforgiveness, resentment—all energies that deplete the Spirit.

Imagine humanity letting go of the attention now spent on the narratives, the talks, and problems that lead to war; the divisions, discord, and hatred.

Would it not make sense that in the pure, unpolluted, clean, and wholesome state of aware Consciousness, there would be a new rising of peace, compassion, love, and joy? All negativity would simply fall away. Humanity would come together, realizing its interconnectedness.

Every situation and event in the world would now unfold in loving compassion and peaceful joy, healing the world in endless ways.

WE ARE SO MUCH MORE THAN
WE BELIEVE OURSELVES TO BE

It is crucial to understand that each of us is so much more than we believe.

You are learning and discovering as you practice here to maintain awareness of a Greater *you* within, healing you and leading to a new perspective, a new way of looking at an outer world with new eyes, a fresh wonder and awe, just as you had as a young child!

You will feel secure and protected with the connection you have to a powerful, vast, and infinite space in which there is no limitation and no lack; no doubt or fear. You are now playing in an open energy field where all is possible!

It is vital to understand that our lives change and transform beyond our wildest dreams when we transcend and move beyond the false, small, limited, ego mind.

A realization and understanding of who you truly are occurs beyond the ordinary, everyday mind, without the need to do anything on your part. A shift, a deeper breath, a deepening peace may occur that is beyond the mind of unwanted thoughts and emotions. It is an energy that is opening— awakening you, more and more, to who you truly are.

You have let go of all that has made you suffer. You have, in that moment, forgiven everyone and everything!

Every moment you spend as your true Self sheds the layers of concepts, opinions, beliefs, and unforgiveness.

In the same moment you commit to knowing your true Self and identity, you are opening the door to many gifts that are beyond anything you can imagine. You are opening to new potentials and possibilities, higher levels of Consciousness, awareness, wisdom, insights, and understandings.

My own path of awakening to my true Self now reveals itself as a profound inner peace that is blissful and more and more euphoric, as I go inward in peaceful aware relaxation. My inner world is calm and peaceful. My writing has taken on this peaceful, almost effortless, energy. While there is still "work" to do, the answers and solutions that I ask for and are given fill me with a sense of trust and reassurance that I am moving forward in the direction of my goal.

Remember that our awareness, where we put our attention, reflects in our outer life of circumstances, situations, and events. The vibrational energy of calm inner peace—free of lesser energies that harm—manifests the same high frequency and vibrational energy in everything we experience.

As you say "I am my true Self," you are affirming your true-identity, and little by little you will release for good the false identity that causes harm in life. All that represents the false identity: emotions of sadness, resentment, anger, disillusionment; all conflict will slowly disappear as you practice realizing and understanding who you truly are. And the key to realizing and understanding who you are is maintaining a connection to your true Self. As you do, you are taking a very important step toward the path of Self-Realization.

Connection in Seconds:

ENCOURAGING A CONNECTION TO YOUR TRUE SELF

When you finish a task and before you start another, say, "I am here in truth and I am listening." In this way, you are encouraging a connection to your true Self and in the same moment recognizing your true-identity. Become still in quiet, non-thought. Learn to engage with your true Self as you connect in silent, quiet stillness.

As you say, "I am here in truth and I am listening," you are encouraging its gifts of guidance, answers, solutions, and inspirational ideas. And you are also accelerating your recognition and understanding of who you truly are.

As you continue practicing, you will sense the Greater self within yourself more quickly and easily, because each time you practice you are letting go of the noise, commotion, and drama of the false self. You are in a powerfully infinite space—spaciousness—of silence.

Keep the connection open to your true Self and be patient. It may take weeks, or even months, to realize who you truly are. You are awakening to truth.

Remember that awakening to who you truly are will come about through experiencing it. The small, ordinary mind of the false ego will never take part in your awakening because of its indulgence in lesser energies like anger and sadness.

The path to self-realization and enlightenment is a path of a lifetime. However, every moment counts! As you do the practices and connections here, there is always something good happening within, and you are accelerating your path even if you do not have a sense of anything happening.

For months on end, I contemplated the natural scene of a beautiful lake in peaceful non-thought. I did not have a sense of anything "happening." However, I did not know at the time that much more was happening within than I could have ever imagined. The valuable gift of a perfect solution to my problem was "developing" simply as I let go of an outer world in the feel-good, peaceful awareness of the beautiful lake I was contemplating. And even still another gift was "developing" as I looked out at the lake view in peaceful silence! A similar lake view that I experienced so many years earlier, manifested into the lakeview I have today from where I write. There is no doubt that the energy of silent awareness in calming peace is powerful!

As you intend to reach, connect, and explore your true Self in peaceful awareness you are awakening Self-Realization. A very powerful thing to do in the only space life truly exists—the present moment.

Chapter Five

LIGHT IS LIFE ITSELF

*Light is the infinite invisible
within that energizes your best life*

When we think of ourselves as only thoughts, emotions, and a physical body, or as we have a conceptual image of ourselves as the person with a career, a member of a family, or the personality self, we have hidden our light within. The vast majority of humanity believes they are their feelings, emotions, thoughts, and body—the stories of their past, the opinions and beliefs they hold, and the personality they present to an outer world.

You, yourself, may identify with roles that are played out in everyday life: the teacher, the student, the boss, the mother, the father, the wife, or the husband; whoever you may think of as yourself.

However, that is not who you are. You are a Greater *you* that can transform your life to create your best life.

We, each of us, are pure Consciousness—an infinite, eternal being. When we tap into this Self—a Self we are calling a true Self—and fill our Consciousness with its vast, limitless and infinite Consciousness, we open to its higher level of Consciousness that is now ours. This higher world, higher dimension, and realm can also be called God, The All That Is, Creation, The Higher Power, the Divine Self, or simply energy. There are many ways of defining this power within that leads each of us to the same path. As we step onto this path, Higher Consciousness flows its limitless and abundant beauty, love, and goodness, into every corner of our life. This is when life takes on a magical beauty and perfection! Remember that Consciousness *is* awareness, so that you are simply opening to a higher level of awareness.

A life-changing step to take on your journey of Self-Realization is to explore this higher dimension beyond the ego, open to its magnetic call, experiencing and knowing it as another part of your life.

In following practices and connections, you will open, explore, and sit in the middle of this enormously magnificent energy of light that is merging more and more with your own light, becoming who you are.

As you continue reading and doing the practices and connections, I will refer to this magnificent power as the Divine Self. You can think of the Divine as energy, if you like. I want to include everyone because this is a real and true, infinite, invisible energy within each of us!

THE UNIVERSAL FLOW
INHERENT IN ALL LIFEFORMS

We may not consider just how similar the natural outer world is to our inner world—the Divine Self we connect with when we are peacefully aware. There is a balance and harmony in an outer world that can be seen, and it becomes obvious as we become more aware of our surroundings.

We see a harmony and balance in the ebb and flow of the ocean, its low and high tides. Its seen again in the changing seasons: the taking away in winter, and the giving back in spring. A harmonic balance continues infinitely, eternally, in every environment all around our globe.

Through the inner world of the Self that you are practicing to *be*, you can live in balance and harmony. As we find it and live it day to day, moment to moment, this harmony and balance will effortlessly create our best life. And it all has to do with tapping into the natural flow of life!

AS ABOVE, SO BELOW, AND AS WITHOUT, SO WITHIN.

This harmony and balance flows deep within every organ of our physical Self—the amazing engineering of our body—without us needing to control its efficiency and natural healing capabilities.

You may have also, at some time, experienced the harmony and balance within a creative pursuit. The beauty that you can feel, see, or hear as you play an instrument, sing, or paint. This is beauty and perfection that soon evolves and becomes effortless!

At some point in life, you may have enjoyed the beauty of a sunrise. Its light easily covering the fogs and mists, creating an intense brightness as if embracing a new day.

In our vocabulary, light has many positive meanings, and is fundamental to every spiritual teaching on earth. We refer to light as wisdom, as being light-hearted and not weighed down with depression and worry.

The life-giving qualities of the sun in our outer world is a most important example of the similarities we share within our inner world.

Our sun is life itself. Life would not be possible without it. You may even agree it is love itself! All life on our planet needs the energy from sunlight to thrive. It replenishes, sustains, nourishes, and soothes, and is mentally and physically healing.

THE INNER LIGHT OF CLARITY AND BRILLIANCE

You are discovering within these pages the natural replenishment, sustenance, nourishment, and soothing qualities that are available within your own inner light!

The light within is real, infinite, and limitless, and is an energy of such magnificence beyond anything you can imagine!

All torment, distress, and misery—all that has caused suffering, anguish, and disillusionment—will simply disappear as we intend to connect and open to the light of Consciousness of our true, Divine Self. All is exposed in the light for what it is— the false ego self. This is the darkness that hinders and obstructs our light.

One of the most important things you can do to transform and change your life for better in every area, is to explore your inner light by sitting and immersing in it and knowing it as another part of your life. As you do this, you are moving beyond the ordinary every day mind—the ego mind. Because you have moved beyond the ego mind and, no longer involved in its commotion, turmoil, and limiting beliefs, you open to the path of Self-Realization. And you awaken.

Moving beyond the limited ego mind is moving into a higher world of light, beauty, and perfection. It is as if in this brilliant light you can see clearly and begin to understand and realize who you truly are.

The realization of who you truly are opens doors to opportunities, qualities of Consciousness, guidance, wisdom—endless gifts and rewards.

Surrender in the energy of light. Immerse and *be* the brilliance of this powerful light. As you do, you are acknowledging that this is who you are and opening to its many gifts.

You may ease into a connection with your true Self in the following:

Connection in Seconds:

LIFTING ABOVE AND BEYOND THE FALSE EGO SELF

Focus awareness on the light in the center of your body, now more beautiful and powerful. Imagine a beam of light descending from above into the top of your head, through the center of your body, to your feet and below. This is your true Self revealing itself. Allow its energy to draw you inward. You may feel its magnetic pull.

Allow your Divine Self to lift you above and beyond the ordinary everyday mind of the ego. Imagine you have reached a mountain top and you are looking out at a higher world and dimension of perfection, beauty, and light. Feel the peace, the silence. *Surrender.* You may call upon a Divine being to assist so that you can lift, expand, and experience this higher dimension of the All That Is, the Spirit, Consciousness Itself that is *you*—your true, Divine Self. Immerse in this immense light like never before, and *be* in the middle of it. You may feel the sensation and freedom of floating as you allow the Divine Self to release a sense of separation you have felt from this higher world of yourself, bringing you into oneness with it.

This is your identity. Your truest, most genuine nature—the Greater You. The You that harmonizes with the beauty and perfection of a matching energetic field that can now be brought into your life through circumstances, events, and situations.

This is an alive Consciousness that is You. It is representative of you in a higher dimension. It is the heart and Spirit of *you*, of all life.

Allow the magnificence that you are, radiate through you. *Be* it and feel it. The moments spent here brings a whole new energy into your life.

Remember that silence is a good way to access this serene and peaceful "space" that is like coming home. As you feel the serene peace, sit in this immeasurable, invisible light that is comforting and soothing. And know it as another part of your life.

Are you ready to identify yourself as the magnificent Self that is beyond the ordinary ego mind?

Connection in Seconds:

SHIFTING IDENTITY TO YOUR DIVINE SELF

Set an intention to identify yourself as the Consciousness of your Divine Self, releasing an identity of yourself as the everyday mind, emotions, and body. Surrender in the peaceful silence.

Immerse and absorb the light of the higher world and dimension of your Divine Self. You are being assisted by Divine beings to help you shift your identity to the Consciousness of your Divine Self. Look out at perfection, light, and beauty, as if you are the identity and eyes of your true, Divine Self. In peaceful calm continue immersing in the middle of this enormous light. Call upon your Divine Self to reveal more of this higher world as who you are so that you may awaken to your true-Identity as an unlimited Consciousness.

Every time you intend a connection and open in this way, you are deepening an awareness of your true-identity—your innermost self, your true, Divine Self, and Source. You are also deepening a connection and opening the energies of a higher Consciousness of the Self. Even if you do not have a sense or feeling of the light of your Divine Self, you are still connecting.

Because as you intend to connect, you are inviting its higher level of light—your light—into your life.

In the same moment you imagine light in your center, you are also inviting your Divine Self into your life!

Little by little, you will feel your brilliant light more and more easily.

I have noticed that as soon as I imagine the light of my formless self, becoming a more brilliant light through my increasing awareness of it, I feel its vibratory presence. And it has become my favorite way to connect.

In the following practice, you are discovering how to use light to dissolve worries, situations, and challenges. As amazing as this may sound, you are using your powerful light (energy) to dissolve and expose the fogs and shadows of conflict of the false self that cause hardship in an outer world. Simply as you imagine your inner light, you are accessing the higher Consciousness of your Self in a higher world, and more and more infusing your circumstances and situations with a higher Consciousness that becomes yours.

Like a laser beam that can cut through anything in an outer world, your inner light can move, cut through, and heal your emotional and mental traumas. In the practices and connections here you will experience this light as a healing light, creating a life that is easier with far less struggle.

In the following practice, you are transforming and dissolving situations with light.

PRACTICE #2

TRANSFORMING YOUR
LIFE WITH LIGHT

1. Inhale and exhale several slow and comfortable breaths. In focused awareness, relax the muscles in your face, your arms, your legs, your whole body.

2. Focus inward on the inner light in your center that is growing in beauty and perfection. You are summoning the energy of your Divine Self simply as you focus on the light in the center of your body.

3. Picture this inner light of the Self, the core of your *Being,* lifting above and beyond the ego self. As you lift into a higher world, imagine you are seeing perfection through the eyes of your Divine Self, at one with the energies all around you. Take in this higher world and surrender in the brilliant light, letting it move through you. *Be* in the middle of this light (energy) of peace, beauty, truth, and perfection. This is who you are.

4. From this higher world of light, you can look down on the thoughts, feelings, and emotions of the false ego and transform every corner of your life.

5. Bring up to the light only briefly a problematic situation, emotion, or relationship, maintaining awareness of your inner being, your light, your Divine Self. Allow a problem or situation to move through your mind. Think of the situation and let it go in a feeling of peace. Watch it dissolve in your light. As it dissolves, your light becomes more brilliant.

6. Bring another situation you would like transformed, or more if you like, one by one, up to your mind, holding it in the light.

7. Know that all you bring up to the light will diminish or dissolve. As you do, you are accessing and bringing back into your life the perfection and beauty that exists in the higher level of light of a higher world.

You have done more than you know. As your inner light transforms situations and circumstances in your life, you understand the great treasure trove you have within to create the life you want.

You are bringing up to the light any troublesome thought or emotion that has kept you stuck and trapped in the energy of feelings that make you feel weighed down. You may get an inspired idea about how to solve a situation or something about it may change, becoming less of a "problem," without you having to do anything. In the same moment that whatever situation is dissolved, it also transforms. You may not even be able to think about the situation when you are in your more powerful and beautiful light!

As you do this practice, you are sustaining awareness of the Consciousness of your Divine Self. A Consciousness that exists in perfection and light, and bringing it into your life to manifest its harmony and balance. From this high and wholesome (holy) state you can manifest and create your best life. You can transform your mind, emotions, and personality.

BRINGING SITUATIONS
UP TO THE LIGHT

If there is an issue in your life—something that you are confused, worried, or uncertain about—bring it up to the brilliant light of your realized true-identity to give you a new understanding—a new realization about what to do—to either dissolve it or, in the clarity of light, perhaps you will find a new perspective that will remove confusion, helplessness, or fear.

The clarity that you gain may come in the same moment you sit in the brilliance of your light, or it may come days or weeks later. Be aware and know that something will change and shift, and will always come to you in a harmonious, balanced way.

It is important not to wonder when or how something in your life will shift and change. Surrender and let it go! Wondering when or how something will change, or being impatient, is to revert to the small, limited, false self-identity—the false ego. Your Presence, your true-identity, in awareness and light will bring about results.

There is nothing more to do. The harmony and balance in your life increases the more you practice inviting and *being* the light of your Divine Self as you have just done. This is a life-changing, transformative step that leads you toward awakening and Self-Realization.

Sustain the high vibrational energy of who you are as your Divine Self! Keep the energy of your light brilliant!

YOU ARE A MAGNIFICENTLY POWERFUL LIGHT

Stay in the light and be absorbed, engaged, and allow it to fill your life, free of the lesser energies of the false ego that have no power at all to create your best life!

In whatever way light comes to you is the right way. You might sense or feel light. As you focus awareness on light, know that you have magnetized it to you, even if you do not sense or feel it.

You can heal within these pages from feelings and emotions that are stressful—that cause you anxiety, emotional pain, and sadness. Imagining light as we are peaceful and aware brings well-being to mind, body, and Spirit.

The path to your magnificence—to become awakened and Self-Realized—is to let go of the fogs and shadows of inner conflict—the stress, the disillusionment, and sadness of the false ego self. This is the darkness that hinders and obstructs your light.

Within these pages, you are clearing, letting go, and releasing the lesser energies and opening to the higher level of Consciousness that makes its way into your life—transforming it, improving it, making it better, and even magical.

As you practice being the higher Consciousness of your Divine Self that is now yours, you are gaining more wisdom and understanding about what to do to improve every area of your life.

Perhaps a relationship needs your attention. As you gain wisdom and understanding, dwelling less on the low energies that no longer serve you, clarity sets in and you now have the tools to transform anything needing your attention.

You will notice that situations that seep up to be fixed or dissolved, once and for all, are little by little gentler and milder and can be remedied more easily. Eventually, there will be no more problems. Or rather, what you once perceived as a "problem," you will not feel anymore because each has been shifted, dissolved, and changed. That is when your experience of life becomes blissful!

Recently, I experienced a very valuable solution of a relationship situation with my daughter when she told me how she felt at certain times in her childhood as she grew up. When she expressed grievances and how she was still remembering, it devastated me. However, in presence, I gave her the space she needed to reveal them. Her complaints were direct and straight-forward.

For a few hours afterward my Consciousness seemed to have left me, because I allowed lesser, dense energies to take control of my mind until the practices I am giving you here relieved me!

I then brought the situation up through the light of my mind, now enhanced by my increased awareness of the brilliant light of my Divine Self. In silent, peaceful awareness, I "looked out" through the eyes of my Divine Self—its highest qualities of beauty, perfection, and light allowing the situation to move through my mind briefly. As I saw the situation dissolve in light, I surrendered, knowing that at the same time it dissolved, it also transformed.

A couple of days later, my daughter told me she did not know why she had brought it up at all. And I told her that I was glad she did because suddenly our relationship is more beautiful, more in harmony and balance than ever. My daughter even expressed amazement when she told me that somehow she had completely forgotten what her grievance was all about! She now tells me how the "problem" she expressed seemed to dissolve, and inexplicably, disappear!

And, I too, experienced the ease in which everything seemed to just fall into place, without either one of us needing to do anything at all. The darkness of this situation was exposed to the light of the powerful Divine Self and it simply vanished and transformed.

There is no doubt that the aware, allowing, and wise understanding that reveals itself in Consciousness is also what helps to transform relationships and situations, because our new awareness does not blame, fault, or judge. In Consciousness, we take full responsibility for the occurrences in our lives and no longer dwell on them, focusing attention instead on the higher vibratory energies of inner peace, joy, and connectedness.

This situation that seeped to the surface to be remedied made me more aware of my relationship with my daughter. The journey of awakening is a slow moving, upward spiral. The spiral slows down with increasing wisdom and insight, as situations and circumstances are honored in our awareness which is our expanding Consciousness.

This is an example of how we are shown those situations we need to remedy in our lives, and as we honor and attend to each, eventually they will all be remedied, giving us an easier life. Our loved ones will "catch" the vibrational energy through resonation and also experience the same magical results.

I, too, grew up with grievances about the way I was brought up. However, today, more so than ever, I understand that any grievance we hold against anyone, whether our parents or a friend, can be dissolved in the realization that *each of us can only act in accordance with the level of Consciousness we hold.*

Forgiveness is then in order. When I remember my parents, now both in spirit, I think or say aloud, "I now understand that you did the best you knew how, thank you!"

Remember that as you practice **being** your inner light with focus and intention in *presence*, in that moment, you have let go and forgiven yourself and everyone—everything that you have experienced in life. In Consciousness everything becomes effortless!

In daily life, you may notice old patterns of thoughts and emotions coming up to the surface, despite the "work" you are doing here. This is a natural occurrence because you have more awareness, and you can see more clearly the patterns of thoughts and emotions that enter your mind.

Learn to accept these more noticeable patterns of thoughts as something you are being shown that needs your attention. Use what you are being shown as something you can bring up to the light. Remember that old, useless, unwanted thoughts and emotions are an opportunity for growth.

The harmony and balance in your life's experiences increase the more you practice inviting, being, and experiencing the light of your true, Divine Self.

Sustain the high vibrational energy of who you are as your true, Divine Self—your true-identity!

Surrender in the energy of light and join and become the brilliance of this powerful light. As you do, you are acknowledging that this is who you are and opening to its many gifts.

This is a light that is comforting and free of inner turmoil. What a relief from the dilemmas and problems of an outer world!

AUTHOR'S MESSAGE

Authors are always seeking reviews so that their message can go out to as many readers as possible. However, we understand your time is valuable.

If you are enjoying this book, please leave a helpful review on Amazon. Even a short review is greatly appreciated.

Thank you!
Darla Luz

Chapter Six

LIGHT'S BRILLIANCE
EXPOSES THE FALSE

Gather the ego scoundrel, the culprit, the crook
Show it to your opulent door
and watch it exposed, then vanished
in your luxuriant light,
now more brilliant than ever

—Darla Luz

THE FALSE EGO

Anything in life that causes suffering, that causes harm, that weighs down our mood, is false, and is the false ego self that most people believe is their identity. When we feel conflict and turmoil within, it is the false living within us, pretending to be us. "The false ego self" has always been and is at the center of every problem—every dilemma—in our world.

As you practice to connect and realize who you truly are, you are being gently lifted out of an identity that most of humanity is living in error.

To dissolve the false that has infiltrated our psyche is to go towards truth! The good news is that it is far easier than you may think to live your truth, as your real and genuine true, Divine Self.

If who we are is easily accessed now, in this moment, how have we lost our way? How did the false takeover and obscure the truth?

As infants and young children, we were pure, vibrant, alive, awareness, living in presence. There was silence within, with no sadness of the past and no worry of the future.

Transfixed, we did not want to miss out on the kaleidoscope of colors and the spectrum of images that passed before our eyes. Our awareness was pure and unbridled, filled with vibrancy, vitality, and sparkle.

In our fresh wonder and awe, we explored a fascinating world that to us held no boundaries, no limits, no self-doubt. The universal flow emanated within. We accomplished any goal without great effort. Our movements seemed orchestrated in a flowing, creative way. We simply set out to accomplish each goal, without the self-doubt, feelings of lack, or fear of failure that is so prevalent in our lives and in the world today.

The true essence of an unlimited Universal flow, available to all life forms on earth, was inherent within.

However, the societal structures we were born into conditioned us since we were children to believe that we are separate in the world from everyone, every animal, and all of nature—all life on earth. This deep subconscious sense of separation has led to fear.

THE FALSE AND DANGEROUS BELIEF

The false belief that we are separate and not connected has led to unkind behavior, cruelty, war, and heartlessness in the world. The challenges humanity is facing today have resulted from this erroneous and false way of thinking, producing immeasurable, colossal danger because of a total disregard and disrespect of our planet and its natural environment, with which we have an undeniable connection and that sustains all life.

The scattered mind we experience as we put attention on an outer world of mass information disrupts and hinders a realization of who we truly are, obstructing an understanding that we are a being who is interconnected with all living forms—a being aware of his or her inner Spirit. And ultimately a being who knows his or her true magnificence within.

Believing we are a separate Self has also led to a belief that we are only our past experiences, thoughts, emotions, and physical body. Much idle time is spent thinking about a hurtful, sad time in the past or thinking about a time in the future with fear. Believing and indulging in the stories and narratives of our past produces unwanted thoughts and emotions that make us suffer. You are coming into the **timeless present moment,** as you practice and connect to who you truly are, *leaving behind a time in the past (sadness) and a time in the future (worry.)*

The false ego is an autonomous entity that fears losing its "life" in your powerful presence. The drama, commotion, and crisis of a painful past or a worrisome future of the false ego are no longer evident when you are present. And you are powerful! That is when the entity, the false ego self and mind, dissolves into nothingness!

IT IS CRUCIAL TO RELEASE THE FALSE SELF AND IDENTITY

You may have thought, along with everyone else, that anxiety,

stress, irritation, and defeatist emotions are normal. I too had this erroneous belief. I heard again and again that life is full of problems and there has always been an implication that we cannot do anything about it.

I can tell you through experiencing the practices and connections I am offering you in this book, I no longer have stress, anxiety, or any kind of lesser energy in my life! It was not always this way, I experienced much mental suffering because I indulged in stories and memories of regret, as well as worry of what the future may hold. There were many moments of unforgiveness as I replayed my past, believing that was my identity.

My realization of my true Self and identity has manifested gifts and rewards, especially the gift of how I feel. And how I feel is truly abundant and wealthy in Spirit! Which is the most important wealth of all. Time and time again, we have heard stories of people who have gained huge material wealth, yet are devastatingly unhappy!

I have noticed that thoughts of the past that once blocked a more joyful experience of life are no longer there. And it has developed through my connection to my true, Divine Self. I will reveal the endless gifts that have manifested in my life throughout this book. These gifts have come about through the same practices and connections I am giving you here, and are available to each and every one of us.

As you practice and connect in this book, you are connecting to your inner Spirit and source, easily and without effort. There is no "work" to do, you need only to have an intent to practice and connect to your Divine Self.

The real "work" will be to remember to have frequent connections throughout your day. Through the practices and connections here, you will be guided to frequently practice and connect with your Divine Self as you go about your day.

Practice makes perfect. As children we practiced riding a bicycle, learning how to swim, playing ball, learning an instrument. And through continuous practice we mastered each, not to mention learning a new language and maneuvering balance and motor skills! As we reached our teenage years, many of us practiced driving. Today, whatever we once practiced again and again has become second nature and easy!

Being your centered, innermost, greater Self can also be mastered through practice, and has untold magical gifts for you.

You may one day realize that daily life is easier, with fewer "problems." You may not even think to link, until sometime later, your practice here to the situations and circumstances that work out in a smoother, more flowing way in daily life.

RELEASING THE EGO
GENTLY AND EASILY

While we need to expose and release what is at the center of our suffering—the false ego self—there is a need to tread slowly, releasing it softly, easily, and gently. Why? Because when we are aligned and centered in the truth of our Divine Self, we are no longer judgmental nor critical, nor have the hidden agendas of the false ego. Only when we are aligned with our inner magnificence—and you will discover your true magnificence as you practice here—can we let go and release what no longer serves us, without resistance, without malaise. We also do not get "rid of" something through effort or hard work. Everything becomes effortless. Through our effortless peace in awareness of our light, the false ego easily disappears and dissolves.

THE SMALL, POWERLESS,
AND WEAK FALSE EGO

The false ego identity that parades itself as your identity is truly powerless. Even though the false ego self seems powerful, it is not. It is weak and small, and while it may seem to be you, it is not! The lesser energies of the false ego mind like anger, resentment, or hatred have no power at all, as well as no light. All lesser energies like fear come from mass human Consciousness and are fleeting thoughts and emotions that have no substance. Fear does not contain the eternal, infinite quality of a higher level of Consciousness, and it can be easily overcome by light.

You cannot manifest a good life from dark energies that do not have the power to create. And you cannot make the sad, hurtful false dissolve into nothingness through the ordinary false ego mind, nor through the will power of this ordinary, small false mind. This small, ordinary false mind, which indulges in drama and crisis, cannot dissolve anything that blocks you from creating a better life because it, itself, is the problem.

You have the power to create the life you want as you transcend and go beyond the false, limited mind. As you imagine light in your centered self, you have in that moment gone beyond the false self.

We give our power away when we believe we are the false self and do not know the magnificence of our true-identity. We give our power away when we are affected by what someone says or does, or when we listen to and act on the continual chatter going on in our head.

We give our power away when we worry about what is happening in an outer world, not realizing our vast, infinite, unlimited, eternal power within. You will discover you have everything you need within you to live a more peaceful, joyful, and effortless life, despite *anything* that happens in an outer world!

If we do not take action to realize our true-identity, we will miss out on an easier life of less struggle. We will miss out on the magnificence of our Divine Self *now*, teeming with energies that can open us to our best life. And we will miss out on the creation of a magical life of gifts that frees us to feel light-hearted, reassured, and connected to all life.

The creation of a magical life comes to a complete stop when we indulge in lesser energies like worry, defeat, anger, or anything that depresses and weighs us down.

These lesser energies are not the light or lightness of our Divine Self—our source and innermost Self. We are then robbed of an easier, more fulfilling life.

Remember that the more we give attention to and feel the anxiety, stress, and fear coming from the false ego—as if it is a part of us, who we are, and our identity—the false ego mind then takes over, relentlessly producing more inner conflict. *Where we put our attention grows in our experience! Whatever we hold in our mind creates our reality.*

As you do the practices and connections, you are often asked if you would like these energies. The reason for this is because of the Universal Law of Freewill. Since we are free to choose how we want to think and feel in our ordinary, everyday lives, it is important to intend and commit to the higher levels of Consciousness of the Divine Self. These are spaces of light and focused awareness so that as soon as we have a thought or emotion coming from the ordinary self, the Divine Self pulls back. Think of the Divine pulling back as out of respect for your capacity for freewill, always remembering the infinite gifts and rewards it truly wants to give you!

I have put enough attention on the false here, and I do not want to create any further experience of it for you.

In following practices and connections, you are exploring and continuing to discover your magnificence! Because that is who you truly are: a limitless, infinite, multidimensional being.

Chapter Seven

YOU ARE MAGNIFICENT: THE ETERNAL REAL AND TRUE YOU

We, each of us, are pure Consciousness; an infinite, eternal being. When we tap into this energy, this Self—a Divine Self—and fill ourselves with its vast, limitless, and infinite energies, we open to its higher level of Consciousness that is now ours. This higher Consciousness flows its limitless and abundant beauty, love, and goodness, into every corner of our life. This is when life takes on a magical beauty and perfection!

A life-changing step to take on your journey of Self-Realization is to allow and open to its magnetic call and explore this higher dimension beyond the ego, experiencing and knowing it as another part of your life.

In following practices and connections, you will open, explore, and immerse in this enormously magnificent energy of light that is merging more and more with your own light, becoming who you truly are. The mind of thoughts and emotions that causes anxiety, stress, and sadness is little by little quieted so that the Self that is truly you is more visible, more evident.

As you immerse in the light of your true Self, you are going beyond the false ego mind and quieting your everyday mind, allowing you to hear the inner guidance—the gentle voice that helps move your life in the direction of your goals and dreams. Even if you do not "hear" the inner guidance of your true, Divine Self, be aware that much more is happening within because this Self is aware of you in every moment and wants to give you everything that you are open to receive. So that as you progress and become the Divine Consciousness of your Divine Self more and more, it will be easier for this Self to give you guidance through answers, solutions, and inspired ideas. And many gifts will flow harmoniously and effortlessly as you understand and realize the infinite, real and true Divine Consciousness that is you more brilliantly than ever.

Your inner light is the real and true, infinite light that uncovers Spirit, becoming more beautiful as your Consciousness is increasingly more aware of it.

However, the Divine light within you has always been beautiful clear and bright. It is your *awareness* that is amplifying and enhancing its power, brilliance, and beauty.

A most important step to take to improve your life in every way is to become increasingly aware, open, and allowing of the

Consciousness of your Divine Self into your life so that its qualities become yours. This will help you gain new understandings and realizations, raising your Consciousness to a higher level of understanding.

It is through this new understanding that your life changes for the better. You are now playing in an energy field that can effortlessly manifest and bring back energies of abundance, well-being, improved relationships, solutions, and answers— infinite gifts coming from an infinite space!

In the following practice, you are increasing your awareness of your true, Divine Self and realizing your eternal nature.

PRACTICE #3

REALIZING THE ETERNAL YOU

1. Allow the light of your Divine Self to make itself known to you even more through your awareness of a light in the center of your body. Let go of an image of your body and simply picture your formless, shapeless Self and increasing inner light.

2. Picture, sense, or feel the light becoming brighter and more beautiful as you are more aware of it. Can you make it even brighter, and more beautiful? Find creative, enjoyable ways to open and allow its visibility, power, and beauty so that you can better recognize and realize it is there.

3. Focus your awareness on a more beautiful, more visible and powerful light, allowing it to inundate and move through your Consciousness, mind, emotions, and every corner of your being. Experience this higher light in a new way as an eternal energy, knowing that as you open more and more and allow it into your life its infinite gifts are yours, creating more harmony and balance in your life.

4. You are now more able to experience the outer world in its eternal rather than its material form. Open to this light of a new understanding, simply surrendering into it.

5. Feel a shift in this light of new realizations and understandings of an eternal, infinite You. These new realizations and understandings are what you bring back into your life to improve all aspects of it.

6. The energetic light that is flooding through you is lessening the separations you have felt and lived in not knowing your true identity. You are now more able than ever to look out at a world with new eyes, understanding an eternal world that is real and true. A world that mirrors the real and true, eternal you.

7. Open to new insights, new understandings, and realizations as you begin to view the world in a new way. Look out at the people and situations. What is real, true, and eternal and what only seems real and true?

8. You are opening to an understanding of your eternal, unlimited nature. This new understanding creates a new reality in your life: greater abundance, more peace and harmony, and new reassurance and trust.

You have done more than you know. This is the light of your Divine Self that is real, true, eternal, and infinite. You are inviting the Consciousness of your true, Divine Self into your life through your aware openness, and creating a more powerful inner light through your focus and awareness of it. Remember that your own inner light has always been and will always be powerful and brilliant.

However, you are increasing its brilliance as you focus your *awareness* on the light of your Divine Self. And, as you gain the qualities of this Self as your own, you open to new realizations and understandings. Your Consciousness is then lifted to higher levels of understandings. That is when an abundance of goodness flows into your life.

In daily life, begin to look at what in the outer world is eternal, has always been and will always be: people, animals, and nature. And take notice of what in an outer world is fleeting, short-lived, and temporary. The material and temporary will recede into the background as you find the true depth and Spirit within all life.

You are beginning to understand your own infinite and eternal nature as well as the infinite, eternal nature of life all around you. The light, the spark, within all lifeforms are more and more evident to you.

You are opening to new understandings as you realize the true heart, Spirit, and Source of all life.

Gifts of abundance in all areas, like finances, love, inner peace, and well-being seem to appear, as if magically. It all has to do with living in higher energies that now reflect into your life.

You begin to understand at a deep level that you are really and truly an eternal, spiritual being, having a human experience.

You will feel calmer about what is happening in an outer world that, in truth, we cannot control.

However, you feel more reassurance and trust to accept and allow each moment to be just as it is, because you now know that you have all you need *within* to create your best life.

Recently, I took a trip with my family to a mountain town, and I intended a connection to my Divine Self in this way—to see and know the difference between what is eternal and what is temporary. The mountain air felt crisp, the sky bright blue, the flowers that lined the streets looked especially vibrant and colorful. The good-spirits of the people we met on the sidewalk filled the air, resonating a high, feel-good vibration. There was no doubt in my mind we are connected, and not separate beings!

By the end of the day, I was truly moved. I saw through the eyes of the Consciousness of my Divine Self—the real, the true—and I felt the eternal, energetic liveliness and fullness of life, in full appreciation!

I encourage you to practice this often because the new realizations and understandings that come about as you differentiate between the eternal and the temporary are profound!

Your heart opens and you find yourself appreciating life more often, which elevates and energizes your vibration powerfully and hence what comes back to you!

You don't have to venture outside of your home to practice seeing the eternal, ever-lasting part of life. You can practice as I do, moment to moment, as you go about your day.

I feel an aware peacefulness when I focus on the eternal, timeless side of life, making me more aware of who I truly am.

I have opened to new understandings, lifting my Consciousness to a new level of understanding. And it has come about through an understanding of the eternal perfect nature of life all around me! I see it in the perfect landing of a little sparrow, its wings falling beautifully and perfectly, like wavy drapes, on its tiny body. I see it in a white gull maneuvering a glide against a bright blue, endless sky. And I see it in the lithe and agile body of a squirrel scampering across my yard.

As you understand and begin to differentiate what is real, true, and eternal and what is only temporary, you gain spiritual awareness. You begin to see a new world with the fresh eyes and wonder of a child. The purity of thoughts and emotions that are experienced through this new realization creates a new reality, changing your life in wondrous ways!

It is through this understanding that what comes back to each of us are gifts beyond measure! A new reality comes into our life! One that opens the heart in great appreciation.

Through this new gift of Consciousness of realizations and understandings, little by little, you may notice improved relationships, greater abundance, and well-being. You may notice you arrive at a place at the right time. This is the Universal flow becoming more evident in your life. Many changes take place as you open with wisdom and discernment to new understandings. There are new potentials, possibilities, guidance, answers—endless, amazing gifts and rewards!

I am, today, experiencing more abundance than ever before, and I know it has come about as a result of gaining new understandings through opening, allowing, and exploring this higher level of Consciousness of the Self.

Whatever I need, whether I am seeking to eat healthier, get more exercise, or I have a question about my writing, or any subject, I am supplied seemingly magically with a random video, random literature that catches my eye, or a thought that seems to come "out of the blue." Help becomes especially evident when it comes to a question about my writing. When we ask for a spiritual gift concerning something that will help others as well as ourselves, the solutions and answers are often immediate!

Recently, I asked an important question about this book. Within minutes, a sentence from something I had been reading earlier caught my eye, as if holding my awareness, and I read it over and over until I realized it was the exact answer I needed! At other times, events that appear to be negative are actually helpful events that move my goals forward!

Be playful and creative in the way you imagine your eternal, Divine Self. There are endless ways to invite it into life. As you become comfortable with the practices and connections here, you may even want to merge two connections into one. Remember that even a connection of a few seconds is very powerful! As you simply focus on the light of your Divine Self, you are inviting it into your life! You are asking for truth to come into life.

Your Divine Self is always trying to reach you, to give you its endless gifts. They are gifts that are special and unique to you because this Self knows exactly what you need!

Does this seem magical?

It is not really "magical" as it is the truth of the energies you can access within. As you practice and connect here, you are holding and sustaining the awareness of powerful energies that you are now activating.

ACQUIRING SPIRITUAL AWARENESS

As you begin to see the difference between what is eternal and what is temporary in daily life, you are acquiring spiritual awareness.

When you look out at the world and begin to take notice of the eternal heart of all life, you realize and understand the interconnectedness of life, the beauty and perfection that truly exists in the world. The feel-good quality you are gaining through spiritual awareness attracts good flowing into your life.

You can now experience the world spiritually aware as you begin to live life in the higher qualities of the Consciousness of your Divine Self, now *your* Consciousness. Your Consciousness is moving into the real and true Spirit of the Divine world.

Your experience of life is revitalized and energized, much like the aware, fresh wonder you had as a child!

You may find yourself appreciating life, as I have, more frequently than ever before! I am thankful and appreciative as I look around at all life that surrounds me. And I am thankful for the trust and reliance I feel, freer than ever of harmful thoughts and emotions that once ran my life.

As you become aware and have new understandings of the spiritual world that exists all around you, and of your infinite, eternal nature, you will gain inner peace, trust, and reassurance, and give less importance and worry to the fleeting temporariness of an outer world.

You may also think of spiritual awareness as becoming aware of your invisible, formless energy. *This Spirit, this invisible form, represents your true, real, Eternal Self.*

Chapter Eight

YOUR MAGNIFICENCE: REALIZING YOUR INFINITE NATURE

Another way you are acquiring spiritual awareness is through understanding the difference between what is infinite and what is finite.

Distinguishing the short-lived, finite characteristic of daily life from the infinite nature of the Self is another part of spiritual awareness. This understanding helps you experience your expanding inner light—a light found in all life—and is now more evident and more obvious to you.

Allow the Divine Self to reveal itself by simply picturing the light in the center of your being.

This is the light of Consciousness of your Divine Self. This light contains an infinite number of qualities of Consciousness.

It is light that reveals abundance. It is Consciousness from a higher world of Spirit—your Spirit.

You may think of this world of Spirit as an invisible, higher energy that can be tapped into in every moment to manifest your best life. It is always available and has awaited your recognition of it.

In a following chapter, more will be said about the invisible energies that exist all around us. We humans are distracted by the material world we live in, without much consideration of the *infinite invisible* power readily available in an instant to make our lives better! We have been led to believe there is lack and limitation.

However, light coming from an infinite world of the Consciousness of your Divine Self—now *your* Consciousness— is infinite and unlimited. This infinite light contains abundance, energy, and light—endless qualities of Consciousness.

Allow the Self to reveal more of its infinite nature, giving you a new realization of it.

Connection in Seconds:

A DEEPER UNDERSTANDING
OF YOUR INFINITE NATURE

Focus on the light that is increasing within you as you become more aware of it, imagining yourself shapeless. Allow the quality of infinity to infuse you with its light. Look out through the perfection of the eyes of your Divine Self and understand the infinite quality of this higher world of Spirit of which you are a part. Open to a new idea and thought of being limitless. Anything you focus on: joy, peace, love, and light, is limitless. Allow the limitless light of infinity to pour through you. Experience it, be it, sit in this expansive light and surrender. Watch this enormous light go out into your outer world of situations. Open and allow this infinite Consciousness of the Self to be a part of your Consciousness.

Unlimited gifts await as you gain a deeper knowing of the infinity that *is* this higher world of Spirit.

Remember that you are "working" with energy here. So that it is okay if you think of this higher world of Spirit as an energy that can be manipulated to influence your life. Most important is the realization of the magnificent energy that is the Self within to transform and improve every area of your life.

As you open more and more to the infinite nature of your being, this Self within you assists in opening a higher path of any choice you may pick, any opportunity that may develop, or any skill cultivated. And these choices, opportunities, and skills are already here, waiting for you to open through the infinite nature that is your Divine Self.

Our experience of an outer world is finite, fleeting, and short-lived. Everything in our third-dimensional earth-plane lives have a beginning and an end: relationships, careers, marriages, and the places we call home. Often, we find ourselves in a descending spiral when anything comes to an end. It might help to know that the natural characteristic of life and the world we live in is finite!

You are practicing *being* a higher Consciousness that is unwavering, stable, never-changing, always available, and is real and true. You need never again feel isolated, bored, or lonely. You have everything you need within you!

In the following practice you are acquiring the quality of infinity so that the limitations you may have accepted dissolve in the aware, conscious, brilliant light of a higher world of Spirit—the Divine Self, which your Consciousness is now moving into. You are aware, open, allowing, and expanding into the quality of infinity in the following practice.

PRACTICE #4

EXPLORING AND EXPANDING INTO THE INFINITE YOU

1. Allow the Divine Self to reveal itself. Sense or imagine a beam of light coming down into the top of your head through your spine.

2. Watch this unlimited, infinite light flood through your being and out into your life. This infinite quality of light can expand limitlessly, moving through all energies.

3. As you focus and become aware of this light, realize that it has within it qualities that are beyond your mind, representing a higher world that is unlimited and infinite.

4. Look out through the perfection of the eyes of your Divine Self at a higher world that is limitless—360 degrees all around you—with no obstacles, no barriers. Rest here, in aware peace, and allow the light of the quality of infinity to flood through your being. Let it become a part of you. Immerse in it, feel it, and *be* it.

5. Allow the Divine Self to enfold you in a deeper realization, a deeper knowing, and an experience of the quality of infinity.

6. Is there an area in which you hold a belief that there is not enough of something? Look at this area through your spiritual awareness, allowing and opening a new understanding of an infinite world. And watch as this area lights up, expands, and is released in the unlimited, infinite light of the Consciousness of the true, Divine Self. If you would like, bring up other concepts and beliefs you may have of limitations to be released in the infinite, unlimited light of the Self.

You have done more than you know. Watch this infinite light of an infinite Consciousness flow out to areas in your life in which you feel lack and not enough supply and abundance. As you move into your infinite nature there is also an infinite component to every quality that becomes yours. As you think of a quality in this space, such as joy, inner peace, or love, you are experiencing its infinite nature and depth.

Every thought you hold in this space expands infinitely. This light within you is all-knowing—everywhere at once—and its expansion limitless and infinite.

Remember that even a brief 10 to 20 second connection is powerful. When you finish one task and before you start another, stop to connect, putting aware focus on your energy of infinity available in every moment.

Is there an area in which you have had on-going emotions of tension or anxiety?

When emotional energies have you in the grip, turn to your inner light as you do the following:

Connection in Seconds:

HEALING EMOTIONS OF TENSION AND ANXIETY

Focus awareness on the infinite light in the center of your body, revealing the light and Consciousness of the Self. This is the spiritual light that can cut through emotions of tension, anxiety, any inner conflict that obstructs you from moving forward in life, hindering your infinite, limitless freedom, harmony, peace, and joy. In aware peacefulness, allow this infinite light to flood your being, and revel in the peaceful depth of infinity.

You have allowed the expansive light of the Self, now *your* expansive light, to dissolve all energies that are limiting.

You have given permission—opened and allowed a new, higher level of an understanding of Consciousness to flood your being. New insights, realizations, and understandings will unfold. It is through this understanding that your life changes for the better. You open to wisdom, improved relationships, opportunities, guidance, and qualities of Consciousness.

Remember that if you believe there is lack and not enough supply in any area of your life, you have blocked an experience of an ability to create the life you want—a life, *your* life, that is truly unlimited in every area. Allow yourself, in every moment, to surrender into the limitless, infinite being that you are! Come into this infinite space.

Connection in Seconds:

DISSOLVING LIMITING BELIEFS

Allow your Divine Self to flood and radiate out through the center of your being a new Consciousness of infinity so that you can release beliefs that limit and hinder your life. Allow the light of infinity to fill your being, and sit in this enormous light for a moment, or as long as you like. Allow this infinity within you that is expanding out further and further to dissolve limiting beliefs as you hold an understanding of your unlimited, infinite nature.

When emotional energies coming from beliefs of not enough supply and abundance surface, turn to your expanding light of infinity. Continue an expansion of this inner light, allowing it to go out further and further, influencing all areas of your life. Realize there is no limit to your new realization of yourself as an infinite being, and you now have a new limitless, expanded experience of infinity.

You are practicing being an eternal, limitless *you* as your Divine Self. You are gaining a new sense of unlimited abundance, and feeling the freedom that comes through a new experience of limitless peace, love, connectedness, and well-being—all qualities that come from an infinite and abundant higher world and dimension that you are engaging with, and that reflects infinity back into your life. Your light expands and expands, going out endlessly. There is no limit to how far it can go. This light of limitless expansion reflects limitlessness back into life.

You have just opened and allowed a new Consciousness of infinity to come into your life. Your Divine Self of a higher, infinite, expanded Consciousness goes ahead and clears a path to new opportunities, abundance, improved relationships, and much, much more!

As the infinity of your being is revealed in your Consciousness more and more, moment to moment, you will open to endless gifts and rewards. With a new understanding of who you truly are, your path of Self-Realization as an awakened, self-realized person—knowing who you truly are—is increasingly clear and unlimited. You can now celebrate a brighter, higher future!

One of my favorite ways to connect is by imagining myself small—surrendered, floating and flying in a vast infinite Universe of stars and planets. I feel the freedom of letting go. As I look out at the infinity that is there as my Divine Self, I immerse in this infinite light of my infinite Self and imagine bringing back this light of infinity into my daily life.

Chapter Nine

MAGNIFICENT YOU: THE INFINITE INVISIBLE ENERGIES WITHIN AND ALL AROUND YOU

Each of us is a formless, invisible Self. Being invisible and formless means there are no hurdles, fences, or barriers that obstruct or hinder any path that unfolds before us. We are unlimited, infinite *beings*, and we can create a life that has no barriers that must be overcome to get what we want in life.

As Einstein said, "Everything is energy." Each of us is energy. The energy that makes up very intricate complex systems that surround our physical body are invisible to us, yet are an energetic life force. This invisible complex system has been known for millennia as a potent power within each human being. This power has nothing to do with what we believe or do not believe, whether we have a spiritual belief or none at all. Each of us possesses the same life force energy—a light, an energy—that is within us, dimmed by an erroneous belief in a false ego identity. A belief that encloses us in the negative notion that there is lack and limitation in life.

In between these pages, you are experiencing and becoming more and more aware of your invisible, powerful, Self within— your Divine Self. And you are gently letting go of the small false ego self that is the cause of all suffering in the world. Living life within the invisible energy of your Divine Self transforms your entire life—one of more inner peace, joy, love, and harmony. That is when door after door opens to a seemingly magical life!

We may not stop to realize just how truly magnificent and impactful the technological invisible energies of phones, computers, and TVs we use daily truly are. They lift, rejuvenate, and excite our Spirit. We can hear someone's voice on the other side of the world. We hold in the palm of our hand a virtually infinite amount of the world's information. We may take for granted and not stop to consider that this technology is derived from the powerful invisible forces in the air, the water, wind, and sunlight. Most of the elements in this amazing technology are also present in our physical body!

WE DO NOT GIVE CREDIT TO THE TRUE MAGIC IN THE INVISIBLE

If we walked into a room and were asked to point out what was in the room, we would probably point out the furnishings, the decorative items, the walls, and floors. Yet, we have left out something that is the most important of all. The invisible space, the air, that makes everything possible. The invisible space that gives us our ability to breath. The invisible space that, because we cannot see it, we do not give it credit or importance! This is the invisible space that is life itself!

In our ordinary, everyday lives we are distracted by the material world that surrounds us. This is the world that is solid, measurable, and visible. As important as the material world and its forms are to us in our everyday lives—houses, buildings, cars, computers, phones—everything is transitory, fleeting, ever-changing, passing through our lives, and rarely staying for long. The material world, in its impersonal, inhuman state has never brought us the true and lasting joy we seek.

However, the invisible energy within each of us, available in every moment, can help us create better material forms, better realities in life. In short, helping us to create our best life, even a life of our dreams!

You can harness and activate this energy within you at any moment because it is always available.

You are doing just that as you practice here. Your Divine Self emanates from your innermost, invisible source energy and is a brilliant and radiant energy of light. As you become *aware* of the Greater *you* within, you link with an invisible energy that is magical and amazing. And it is available now, in this moment, to lift, excite, and soothe your Spirit, very much like the technological energies experienced in an outer world.

Within these pages, you are discovering how to connect with this invisible energy to capture its powerful energies of omniscience, omnipotence, and omnipresence. The energies that are all around you *now,* that are infinite intelligence, all powerful, and everywhere at once. You are discovering the real, the true, and the eternal that awaits your recognition of it.

Everything you need is within you. There is nothing to seek because you already are.

There is no reason for you to ever again feel down! There is a life force energy you can connect with in an instant and feel its unconditional love, companionship, peaceful calm, and joy.

The truth is, you are a limitless, powerful, and magnificent being that can create your best life possible.

In ordinary, everyday life, you are expressing as an individual "person." However, you are much more than just the person that came into this physical existence and expects that existence to end.

You are energy that continues eternally, endlessly. You can tap into your infinite, eternal energy through your awareness. This energy is like a safe-haven, a shelter from lesser energies that harm like fear, sadness, and anxiety. As you are aware in this infinite "space" the lesser energies that harm dissolve into nothingness. This infinite energy exists in a higher dimension of perfection and beauty, bringing back to you the same flowing perfection and beauty into every corner of your life.

This invisible energy within you can free you of all that has caused you to suffer. As you become increasingly aware of it, your Divine Self is the highest energy of light and will now shine more brightly than ever within you. Remember that everything around us is energy. The way you are "working" with energy here is simply resting in peaceful awareness as you go inward.

In an outer world, something easy and effortless seems counterintuitive to how we believe a goal or anything that we want is accomplished.

However, the journey inward is simple and uncomplicated. You are doing much to improve your life as you go inward in restful relaxation and peace! A most extraordinary thing happens as we discover the invisible energy of our true, Divine Self, sit and immerse in its light, and explore it as who we are. Because the invisible energies within us are infinite and unlimited, once we explore the space of the invisible energies of this Self, we bring back an infinite and limitless quality to whatever we experience in our everyday life. This is when life becomes extraordinary!

In the following practice, you are experiencing the infinite invisible *you*.

PRACTICE #5

YOU ARE AN INFINITE
INVISIBLE LIMITLESS BEING

1. Imagine a radiance that comes from the center of your being. Let go of a sense of your physical body, imagining yourself as an infinite invisible energy of light, as if your centered self is formless and shapeless and made up of pure light.

2. You are being met by a Presence, a light that is inviting and loving, enveloping you into itself. There is no end to the light of your Divine self in the core of your being. You might imagine yourself small as you fall into the infinite space of this light letting go in peaceful, trusting, surrender. Feel the shift in your Consciousness of a deeper peace, a deeper awareness.

3. An awareness of this infinite light within you is growing stronger. You now know you can live in two worlds, your everyday world and your inner world.

4. Call upon and allow this very real part of you—your Divine Self—to reveal and make itself more known to you, more evident so that you can have more awareness of it in your daily life. Imagine the light of this very real part of you

flowing out into every situation in your life. Feel a deeper shift in your awareness. You have opened the vibrational frequencies, the energies that help you maintain a connection with a very *real* part of yourself.

5. You are more receptive, more alert and aware of the energies coming from the Divine Self that flow down through the top of your head into your spine and out into your life.

6. You have opened to many gifts this very real part of your Self brings into your life: peace, harmony, love, joy, including guidance, answers, solutions, and much more.

You have done more than you know. Your Divine Self is always aware of you and truly wants to offer you the most beneficial energies that make your life better, increasing its harmony and balance. All that has made you feel weighed down, sad, anxious, and angry will simply dissolve in the increasingly clear light of your Divine Self.

You may feel a shift—a greater peace, a deeper breath—as you imagine that you are being magnetically drawn in, as if embraced and supported by a loving presence that assists and strengthens its connection to you. Experience this powerful connection, even for a moment.

Feel the strength here of a greater awareness of peace, a letting go and surrendering in a space that is inviting and caring.

Open to the energy that this Self within yourself always has available. Allow it to increase its contact with you. Call upon this very real part of you to make itself more known, more visible, and real to you so that you may experience its good flowing into your life.

Contact with this very real part of you changes your life in amazing ways in which peace and harmony, guidance, abundant supply, improved relationships, and many more gifts manifest in life. Maintain a consistent and steady connection to the infinite invisible within.

You are awakening an awareness of an invisible world alongside your everyday world. You are giving permission for more contact with this Self within yourself that is the cause of all that materializes in an outer world, and is opening the door for pure good to flow into your life.

As you imagine your brilliant, centered, powerful inner light, you are allowing your Divine Self to assist you in turning inward and upward and away from energies that do not move life forward.

As you imagine this light shining brightly through every circumstance and event in your outer world, you are creating a wondrous life that will take place in days, weeks, or months.

You are shifting and changing, gaining focused awareness of the powerful inner world of your Divine Self. Allow it to become more magnetic, more present in your life, so that you may have a consistent connection with it, and claim its Consciousness and its qualities—its gifts—as your own.

REALIZING YOUR SPIRITUAL POWER OF TRUTH AND WISDOM

Open and allow more awareness of Spiritual Power, a realization of your infinite invisible truth. Knowing the truth of your identity in wise discernment will help you turn away quickly from the impersonal energies that prevent you from creating your best life.

Are there activities, interests, or habits that you would like to release easily and quickly? Allow this Self to help you turn inward and upward more often so that you can easily turn away from activities and actions that no longer serve you.

Connection in Seconds:

STRENGTHENING YOUR ABILITY TO
TURN AWAY FROM LESSER ENERGIES

Allow your Divine Self to strengthen your ability to sustain contact and turn inward and upward, dissolving the pull of thoughts and activities of a lesser energy. As you focus on the quality of *spiritual power*, the wise understanding of truth in your life, relax and allow the Divine Self to assist you in connecting to this power. The awareness of spiritual power helps you let go of the illusions and fantasies that come from the lesser, weak energies of inner conflict, fear, sadness, anxiety, and tension. Light is moving out from the infinite invisible in your center. Imagine this as the infinite invisible light and wise spiritual power of the Self that is moving through all energies in your life, lifting, opening, matching, harmonizing the good and dissolving what no longer serves you.

As you focus on the quality of Spiritual Power, you are understanding more and more the truth of the infinite Universe of which you are a part. The finite trait of an outer world is receding into the background, making it less important in daily life. Allow and watch this powerful light of new realizations and understandings, increased wisdom, and a new ability to turn away from low energies. Watch as it cuts, moves through, and dissolves all low energies that create havoc in life. You are claiming a Divine Consciousness that is increasingly helping you live in your inner spiritual world as well as your everyday outer world in a more harmonized way.

You are now more able than ever to simply observe a divided world in conflict and not become involved, feeling great strength within your inner world.

OPENING TO A NEW AWARENESS OF YOUR SELF AS A VASTER, MORE COMPLETE, AND WHOLE BEING

The infinite invisible that is your Divine Self consists of a vaster and more immense energy than you have allowed into your Consciousness up to now.

As you open and allow the vaster infinite Consciousness that represents a more whole and complete you, you open to many more gifts, accelerating and quickening your path of awakening and Self-Realization.

In the following practice, you are opening, allowing, and reaching a vaster, infinite Self.

PRACTICE #6

EXPANDING AWARENESS OF YOUR VAST, INFINITE INVISIBLE SELF

1. Imagine waves of light going out from your center like waves that spread out further and further when a pebble is thrown into a pond. These waves of light are coming from within you. It is your infinite invisible Consciousness that spreads out through your body, emotions, and mind, influencing all energies as it harmonizes, opens, and lifts.

2. Focus attention on your inner light, and at the same time focus attention on your infinite, more expanded Consciousness moving outward influencing more and more energies.

3. You may notice that as you put awareness on the Divine Self of an expanded Consciousness within you, the rays of light, now stronger and more beautiful, move out further and further, affecting and impacting all energies more powerfully.

4. Your Divine Self is offering you a gift of Divine Consciousness. Imagine a door opening. You are being offered a gift of awareness that has not been available to you until now. You are invited to become more aware of

many more dimensions of which you are a part. As you go through the door, simply open and relax in calm inner peace and receive this gift of awareness, of Divine Consciousness.

5. Luxuriate in this rich peaceful spaciousness and surrender. Something is more whole and complete within you. There is a deeper understanding of who you are.

6. This gift from the Divine Self of a new expansion of your Consciousness allows you to be more aware of the expanded, infinite invisible that is *you*. Experience the abundant and vast richness in this space of more awareness of your vaster, more complete, infinite Consciousness.

7. In this rich space, allow the Divine Self to open you to sense, know, or feel in a deeper way new parts of your Consciousness. You have opened to qualities you can express, more than ever, of new attitudes, insights, and ways of thinking.

You have done more than you know. You have opened to an increased awareness of your Divine Self, the multidimensional infinite being that you are. This increased awareness of who you are will accelerate your path of awakening, open you to new potentials, and increase the qualities of Consciousness you demonstrate in your relationships and in all that you do.

Through this gift, a new part of the Consciousness of your Divine Self is revealing itself more than ever before.

You are expanding your awareness of a more complete and whole (holy) you.

Are you ready to open to knowing more of who you are? Are you ready to open to the Self of a higher dimension—the multidimensional you? To know and experience a higher dimension of a higher frequency?

In the following you are being asked if you would like a greater expansion of your awareness.

Connection in Seconds:

OPENING TO THE GIFT OF AN
EXPANDED CONSCIOUSNESS

Imagine waves of light going upward and out through your mind, emotions, and body. These waves of light are coming from the infinite invisible energies within you. You are being asked by Divine beings and your Divine Self if you would allow an even wider space to be opened for you of the door you just stepped through. As you emerge on the other side of the door, you will be a different You. As you experience this wider space, you may feel a sense of completeness—of unity—as if it is all you need in this moment. It may come to you as a deep inner peace, a deep silence, or through a sense of a flare-up—an explosion. There is nothing to do but relax and open to the rich energies available in this space. The gift of knowing yourself as a more complete, whole Consciousness is now yours.

The gift of a more whole and complete *you* changes your life, reflecting the higher energies of a higher dimensional *you* in every corner of your life.

The expansion of your awareness, your Consciousness, is available in every moment. All potentials and qualities of Consciousness that are ready to open become yours.

As I wrote this book, I have lived the practices and connections I am giving you here. I can tell you with great certainty they work! I feel a new enthusiasm and joy as I start my day. It was not always this way. The thoughts and emotions, the ordinary stresses, and anxieties that thread through daily news and commentaries, I no longer *feel*. I am an observer, and that is all. I am aware of my inner light, now stronger than ever, and in full recognition of the entirety and fullness of who I am.

There *are* moments when I become aware of negative thinking! However, I use these practices and connections to turn away quickly and much more easily than ever. And through focused awareness of these energies, *you too can* now turn away quickly and easily from lesser energies that harm.

These energies are real! There is no need to demand or try hard to bring them into your reality. As you live in your expanded Consciousness, everything that occurs comes to you effortlessly rather than you having to struggle and push for something you want. Consciousness allows you to work from the effortless inside out rather than from the *"trying and laboring"* outside in! You can now feel great compassion for the endless uphill battles the ordinary false self has experienced in life. Have great love and appreciation for this self that has brought you to this point!

Every time you come into this space and imagine a door opening and you enter, you increase awareness of the wholeness and completeness of your being. Past, present, and future come together with no separation. You are becoming aware of the multidimensional, infinite Self that you are. Expanding your awareness of your infinite, eternal and vast Divine Self, like you just did, affects your life in an infinite number of good ways. You are taking a quantum leap, dramatically increasing your energies and accelerating your path into light, changing your life in amazing ways. There is more reason than ever to feel and express new vitality and enthusiasm for life!

Connection in Seconds:

PAST, PRESENT, AND FUTURE
COMING TOGETHER IN ONENESS

A door opens, and again you step inside feeling or sensing the peacefulness in this abundantly potent space of a higher dimension. Your Divine Self is showing you your whole and complete Self of a higher dimension so that you can be more aware of who you are and feel inspired to explore your vast infinity. You may experience a shift now or in days or weeks to come. All parts of you are coming together in this rich space as one: past, present, and future.

Recently, I wanted to purchase an item and realized I was short fifty dollars. I said simply, "I need fifty dollars," hoping that my inner teacher and guide, who has always come through in good and amazing ways, was listening. I *always* acknowledge everything sent to me in great appreciation. *That same day*, I picked up my mail and opened an envelope from a credit card company. To my amazement, there was a check for fifty dollars! I had completely forgotten that, about a week earlier, I had opted to receive a check rather than apply payment to my credit card.

While this may seem to be a trivial occurrence, I am still always amazed at the gifts and rewards we receive in an effortless way as we open and allow a more expanded Consciousness! This experience is a good example of the past, present, and future coming together in oneness and no longer separate, which is revealed through these energies.

Maintain an awareness of your expansion of Consciousness so that you can know your whole, completely integrated Self in a stronger way.

Chapter Ten

YOU ARE A PURE,
CLEAR ENERGY OF LIGHT

The light within you is stronger and more beautiful with every connection. Every time you connect to the light of Consciousness of your Divine Self—imagine or sense it—it becomes stronger, steadier, and more stable. It is aware of you and always responds to your call. This is the Divine Self within that *is* your energy and light.

PRACTICE #7

REALIZING THE PURE
CLARITY OF YOUR INNER LIGHT

1. Notice your breath is deeper and more relaxed, taking you to peaceful calm quickly so that you can now, more easily than ever, sense the light within you that is stronger and more beautiful with each connection.

2. Your inner light is growing through your increasing awareness of it. More and more light is going out and coming back to you. It is a light that moves and cuts through anything. It is pure, consistent, unwavering, touching all energies with its clear, wholesome, unpolluted energy.

3. This Conscious light is responding to you in this moment and is offering the gift of a more illuminated light. Imagine or picture a luminous light coming from the center of your head. This light is dissolving the mental plane of thoughts, emotions, and misperceptions. It is radiant as it absorbs into the light coming from your center. Imagine its radiance like a flame being absorbed into a radiant sun, its brilliance illuminating out infinitely.

4. Feel the strength and stability of this light as it moves through you, clearing all energies that are ready to fall away so that they no longer obscure your path to a better life. In any moment you may ask your Divine Self for a more illuminated light of clarity because it is always aware of you and always responds to your call.

You have done more than you know. An illuminated light helps you move forward in clarity, affecting all energies around you in a good way. Feel the stability and strength of a more powerful and beautiful light that you have created. You are gaining awareness of all the light you can hold. It is fine if you do not sense it or feel your inner light, because it is always a part of you, always aware of you. Remember that this is a conscious light that is becoming more magnetic, more real, the more you become aware of it.

The light of clarity is an alive Consciousness. By focusing on it, it responds to your call. As you have called it to you, it has grown more powerful and beautiful, and you have become more aware of it in your daily life. As you commit, allow and open to being an illuminated light in your daily life you open to many gifts and you become a light for others.

You are growing more peaceful, more in harmony with who you truly are. Simply as you put focused attention on your breath, a gateway to your inner being, it feels deeper and more relaxed, so that you can now connect with the light that you are more easily than ever.

Call upon your Divine Self for assistance to help you become even more aware of the light within, so that you can be integrated and in integrity with its pure, wholesome, genuine, real, and true energy.

Your Divine Self goes ahead, clearing the best possible path in life through your increased clearer light that you are open to and allow into your life.

This is the light of the Self that is unchangeable, unwavering—always has been and always will be. It is like coming home to its peaceful tranquility: the deep roots, foundation, and core of your being.

Connection in Seconds:

SHEDDING MORE LAYERS THAT
HINDER AND OBSTRUCT YOUR LIGHT

Ask your Divine Self for even more inner light. The Divine Self will always gladly give as much light as you are open to receive. In fact, it will give you anything that you are ready and open to receive. You may ask a Divine Being for assistance in shedding the many layers that hinder and obstruct your light. There may be untruths that you have agreed to. There may be certain ways of thinking you are holding onto. Or you may be taking in fearful and unproductive mass conscious collective thoughts. You are now ready to allow as much light as you can hold to radiate from your center. Imagine more and more light going up through your mind, dissolving all mental thoughts and emotions that no longer serve you. Your brilliant, strong, and steady light is shining more brightly and more visibly than ever before.

Maintain this clear light in your daily awareness, play with how much more beautiful you can make your inner light. Is it a rainbow arching up toward higher worlds and dimensions? Is it iridescent, shimmering, and sparkling? Remember that what we feel, either light-hearted or heavy, and who we are within will appear in our outer world of experiences. Creating a beautiful light within attracts beautiful experiences. The light of your Divine Self, *now your light,* is never affected by lesser energies. However, it can affect all energies—clearing the space all around you and creating a path of greater order, calm, and harmony.

This light maintains clarity so that those activities, thoughts, and relationships that you know to be detrimental will disappear in the clarity of your light, as you gain increasingly clear realizations and understandings. As you surrender into the clear light of your Divine Self better and better outcomes will naturally without great effort appear in life.

Call for even more clarity in the following connection.

Connection in Seconds:

BEING A CLEARER AND CLEARER LIGHT

Put aware focus on the center of your being. Many Divine Beings are asking if you would like to clear the energy and open the space all around you so that you can be a clearer and clearer light. You can, if you'd like, call upon Jesus Christ, your guide, beings of light, or your Guardian Angel to help you clear the space so that you can become a clearer light. You are being lifted above and beyond lesser, harmful energies. Picture your light clearer than it has ever been, moving through your mind and out further and further through all energies. Notice your radiance increasing as it dissolves the detrimental energies and emotions of cravings, longings, and yearnings. You are a clearer and clearer light knowing your clear, higher path and less affected by limiting emotions.

A most important thing to do is to maintain your clear inner light. Become more aware of the light in your center. And, more and more often, *be* the harmony and inner peace you are experiencing as a clearer and clearer light.

Remember that it is important to maintain an expression of the integrity of your clearer, purer thoughts and emotions. There are many instances in daily life that will give you the opportunity to express higher thoughts and actions.

A desire for a material object may cross your mind. And what you need and deserve will become clearer as you embody and express your true-identity, your Divine Self, and understand its power and its limitless supply and abundance. So that what you actually get is even better than what you can even imagine! Stay connected so that you can cultivate the clear and true expression of the Self moment to moment!

A good way of connecting quickly to your innermost Self is through picturing a light coming from your spine and radiating out further and further, aware of its unlimited and infinite illumination, affecting all energies in a good way.

Maintain the clarity of your light so that you are no longer affected by the thoughts and emotions of a lesser energy.

Connection in Seconds:

BEING AN ILLUMINATED LIGHT

Relax in silent awareness, *being* your illuminated light. Think briefly of what feels unconstructive or negative in your life: whether relationships, activities, or habits. Watch the clear and pure illuminated light move up through your mind and emotions, and out beyond—infinitely—knowing it can move and cut through all energies. Feel the freedom and the letting go of all that no longer serves you.

A new illumination has opened stability and strength to help you turn away from that which is detrimental and useless. You are sustaining a clearer, purer state of Consciousness.

Many more gifts are in store for you as you connect, explore, and become the qualities of your clearer illuminated light of your Divine Self. A gift may be as magically magnificent as an improved relationship with a loved one. Or it may be as small as an idea coming through your mind, helping you to do a chore more quickly and efficiently.

While a deeper connection to source energy has manifested more feelings of inner peace, joy, love, and connectedness, I always acknowledge these moments that reveal a flow of perfection and beauty, saying thank you, thank you, thank you! I know that a clear mind that is free of lesser energies that weigh down the psyche brings about higher thoughts like appreciation and gratitude and its accompaniment—joy!

Clarity of mind also promotes harmony and balance. I have noticed a multitude of times when my timing to be someplace is perfect. Something as simple as a call received just as I have finished a task reminds me that through pure, clear energy, goodness flows. Always accept the flow of life as it presents itself in great appreciation.

Chapter Eleven

TRUTH:
YOUR MAGNIFICENCE
IS REVEALED THROUGH
YOUR LUMINOUS LIGHT

Consider and appreciate all the light, growth, and transformation you are experiencing as you connect to your Divine Self. In the following practice, you are becoming aware of an even more radiant and clear light within, expanding your Consciousness and illuminating through your increasing light all energies that are ready to awaken. Your light has always been a clear, bright light and is now enhanced through your connection to your Divine Self of a higher world and dimension that is increasing, and will now, change your life.

PRACTICE #8

INCREASING AWARENESS
OF YOUR RADIANT LIGHT

1. Become aware of the growing light in the center of your being. If you would like, ask your Divine Self for assistance to increase growth and transformation. As you do, you are moving into higher levels of increasing light.

2. Your expansion of clear, radiant light is more evident and more and more a gift to others and to yourself. You are realizing that every gain you make as you expand your Consciousness, sustain an illuminated light, understanding who you truly are, is a gift to others.

3. Open to this understanding as you imagine you are pure light, letting go of a sense of a physical body. Your Divine Self is aware of you as you focus on your inner light, and is opening and assisting you in every way so that you can know the infinite levels of light available to you, increasing your growth and transformation.

4. Your light is growing brighter, more and more illuminated. You are expanding into infinite light that has no boundaries—no limits—leaving behind a limited reality.

You are opening to a vast universe of Consciousness and light. You *are* this light.

5. Imagine a path opening, clear and lit up, more visible than ever, increasing your awareness of an awakened, enlightened state of Consciousness.

6. From this higher space, reach out to the Self living in the fourth dimension and watch this Self reach out to you enveloping and merging with your limited self of a third dimension. Both selves create an enormous light.

7. In this higher level of Consciousness in which the energies like joy, harmony, insight, love, and inspiration are boundless, you may ask your Divine Self for an increase in your ability to express and *be* the higher level of qualities of Consciousness. As you ask, know that it is yours in this unlimited, infinite, luminous light.

You have done more than you know. You are increasing an understanding of the Self—yourself—as a multidimensional being. More aware than ever of your clear, enormous light, merged with the Self in a higher dimension. You are a massive light, symbolically able to see 360 degrees infinitely in all directions. Your light has expanded, transcended, and gone beyond the ordinary self of this dimension, crossing into a boundless, limitless fourth dimension in which there are no barriers or limits.

This light that you are, is not bound by space or time. You are tapping into the higher, vast, infinite energies of your Divine Self that are limitless, transferring this limitless quality into your life. The unlimited Self of a fourth dimension is reaching out to the limited self of a third dimension, creating a powerful light.

Everything comes together as one here: past, present, and future, as well as the merging of the limited third dimensional personality self and the higher fourth dimensional *you*. This merged, immense light helps you see your path more clearly. This is an immeasurable light that goes beyond all barriers, lifting and stimulating all energies of potential that are ready to surface.

Energy after energy is expanded and awakened here, embracing all energies that are dormant and waiting to be activated. All energies that do not align with this higher level of light are falling away.

Infinite Universal qualities are drawn and magnetized into the luminous light that is *You*.

This is a beautiful and radiant light that awakens new qualities of potential and ability.

The gift of your expansion into the light of your Divine Self is one of the greatest gifts you can give to everyone around you! The clearer and more radiant your inner light, the more you can offer others.

The fulfillment I feel from having written my first book, and now my second, to help *you* create and live your best life, has been truly extraordinary for me. I do not believe I could have accomplished writing the books from the "will power" of my ordinary self. The will power coming from the false ego identity that becomes frustrated, impatient, and fearful when something goes wrong! It has come from the more effortless will of my true Self! It is the truth of what the genuine, real, and authentic Self loves to do. It is the I AM that is driving the effortless true and real qualities of a higher level of Consciousness.

Everyone of us can open to an experience of creating something that we genuinely and truly love to do! We are each a unique being, so that what each of us experiences is our own genuine and unique set of desires. As you become increasingly aware of the luminous light of the core of your being, everyday situations and experiences that once distracted you, blocking you to move forward with more joy and enthusiasm, gradually fade. You are becoming more aware of the Self, of a higher world and dimension, gaining peaceful awareness and harmony, and knowing the increased potentialities that you can open and allow into your life, creating a wondrous life!

Connection in Seconds:

ASKING FOR GUIDANCE AND SUPPORT FROM YOUR AWAKENED SELF

Picture your third dimensional self merged with your fully awakened Self of a higher dimension. In this space of an immense energetic light, you may ask for guidance on what steps to take next. You may ask to live more aware and sustain the higher spaces of your Divine Self. Or you may ask for an increase in your capacity for growth, progression, and transformation. Simply ask, relax, and open to receive. You have triggered and activated infinite energies, creating positive changes in your life.

You have done much to change your life in positive ways. You have opened to a higher probable reality and potential, and asked for an increase in your capacity for growth. Much activation takes place as you explore your true, Divine Self of an increased illuminated light.

LIVING THE LIGHT OF TRUTH

Truth in all areas of your life unfolds as you set an intention and open to truth.

As you open to truth, you will understand the limiting beliefs and illusions you have accepted—that problems are normal, that life is difficult, that your life is limited—and shown what is real and true, setting you free. Opening to higher truth awakens you to a wise understanding of the endless gifts your Divine Self truly wants to give you like Self-Realization, guidance, unconditional love, and qualities of Consciousness.

Truth may come about through a deep feeling of peace, a recognition, a knowing realization, or in any other way. In all areas of your life, all that is false simply falls away as you live in your increasingly brilliant light of truth.

In our world today, the false ego is a keeper of many untruths. Living and *being* truth in our daily lives frees us. We are living in truth the same moment we are aware and focused on our breath, our light, our inner being. The false has fallen away.

In the following practice, you are setting yourself free.

PRACTICE #9

LIVING IN THE LIGHT OF TRUTH

1. Set an intention to become aware of higher truth in all areas of your life.

2. Open and become receptive to your Divine Self of guidance, wisdom, unconditional love, and qualities of Consciousness that it offers in every moment. In this moment, you are awakening to a higher truth.

3. Affirm an intention for a greater knowing and understanding of your Divine self, as well as an acceptance of the gifts this Self has for you. Your light is expanding, reaching higher and higher energies of light, of dimensions. You are pure, focused, aware light.

4. This light is *you.* Your true, Divine Self is aware of your intention. Divine Beings are with you, gently and harmoniously lifting layers of untruths that you have accepted and have held you back from moving forward in life, exposing a clearer light of truth. Your light is expanding its brilliance and clarity so that truth can be revealed in all areas of your life.

5. You have opened a new, powerful energy of truth. Feel it, sense it, *Be* it! You are more focused on the light within that takes you upward and out infinitely. You are more than ever realizing yourself as a limitless, multi-dimensional Being. A new Consciousness is yours.

You have done more than you know. Living in the light of truth will set you free from limitations you have accepted in life. This higher truth will open you to Self-Realization, to knowing who you truly are, your genuine true, Divine Self. This light of truth opens you to endless gifts including wisdom, self-love, and being a light for others.

You are opening to truth from an ordinary third dimensional being to a multidimensional being. You are opening and connecting to higher dimensions of truth, so that you are better able to see the world around you in the aware and wondrous way you opened to it as a young child. You are recognizing the truth of who you are at more levels: a multi-dimensional being.

The energies that create a better life for you are now in place. You are an observer of life, not taking life so seriously because you know you have everything within to create the life you have always wanted.

The light of truth is the driving force of your true, Divine Self. This light of truth is what reveals your authentic, genuine, and very real Self, leading to truth in all areas of your life. In the following connection let go of all energies, all the illusions that you have agreed to that are not yours.

Shine this light of truth of a higher dimension in an area in your life in which you would like greater truth.

Connection in Seconds:

SPOTLIGHT ON TRUTH

Put the spotlight of truth in an area of your life and notice what changes in your attitude, perception, or in the situation itself. As you change your Consciousness, situations change also.

You may reach up and embrace this very real light of truth. It is as if it is solid. You may ask about your life, your purpose. You have little by little lost the image of yourself, your physical body. You are seeing and knowing the Greater you, the Self that is shapeless and formless, able to reach higher and higher as you live in the lightness of the heart of a higher world.

This light opens the real, the true and the beautiful.

As you look over your life, is there anywhere in which something is no longer aligned with the truth of every part of your being? Is there an activity, a relationship, that you would like to harmonize with who you are becoming?

Connection in Seconds:

ASKING FOR A TRUTH TO BE REVEALED

Ask and open to a truth to be revealed to you. As you shine your luminous light, open and be receptive to what comes back. In this moment, you may have an insight as you open to this gift of truth, or it may come to you weeks from now. Your Divine Self is made up of truth. Feel it, open, accept, and surrender in this light of truth.

The gift of truth from your Divine Self is a most valuable gift.

Call upon the energy of truth at any time, so that you can know more of who you are, and love and appreciate yourself more than ever. You may ask for new awakenings, understandings, and truths.

You are awakening in a deeper way to truth. Call upon the energy of truth throughout the day so that you can remove the concepts, beliefs, and illusions.

Setting an intention to the truth in all areas of your life is an expansion on the path of awakening. An awareness of truth will free you from the limitations you have accepted as you have lived life with a false ego identity. The untruths of beliefs, concepts, and perceptions that you are only your personality, your mind, thoughts, emotions, the shell of a physical body, and your past, have fallen away.

The concepts and thoughts that hold you back and weigh you down are dissolving. You are opening to unimaginable gifts because everything that you feel, think, and carry out in life is now truthful light. A truthful light that holds only positivity, giving you a lightness in heart in all you say and do.

As you become aware of higher truths, you become a light for others. You are gifted with a knowing of higher truths.

My experience in living consciously aware of my Divine Self, a power of truth, has improved every part of my life!

I am experiencing improved relationships, more joy, inner peace, love, and its closely related energy of compassion!

A desire to organize my personal space feels easy, effortless, and flowing as I tidy-up, pick-up, and put away. The moment-to-moment connection with my true identity, free of lesser thoughts and emotions, has brought about almost magically more self-discipline.

You may notice that everything that you do may simply feel more effortless. You may not even realize until later that your life has changed for the better, as you have practiced and connected here. You may notice improved relationships, improved finances, increased well-being, less conflict, and being at the right place at the right time.

We are all aware that the world is increasingly complex. However, as you practice here, you are gaining awareness, understandings and realizations, inspirations, opportunities, and solutions. Living in the light of your Divine Self and identity will bring about more calm inner peace than you have ever known. Little by little, you will feel a reassurance, as I do, that all is well within your own inner world, and hence, all is well in your personal outer world!

Remember that whatever you focus on in this expanded, illuminated light of truth is limitless, infinite, and abundant. There is a never-ending, infinite supply of joy, inner peace, love, compassion, understandings, and realizations as you hold these spaces in your awareness.

Believe in your powerful magnificence, because that is who you are—in truth! Come to the energy of truth often so that you can move and cut through the illusions and deceptions.

The depths of your pureness and goodness, without lesser energies, are limitless and abundant. You feel more vibrant, peaceful, loving, compassionate, and joyful! And as you are aware of a deeper, limitless, sense of your Self, everything in your life becomes limitless and abundant. This means that all situations, circumstances, and even relationships that you experience in your everyday life take on a limitless and abundant nature, bringing you a flow of goodness into your life and the feelings of reassurance and trust that all is well.

Chapter Twelve

THE INFINITE ENERGY
OF LOVE WITHIN YOU

YOU ARE THE ENERGY OF LOVE

Your true, Divine Self, your innermost Self and source is connected to the energy field of love that surrounds you in every moment. In the following practice, you are opening as never before to the energy field of love that will expand and awaken your heart center, opening you to its flow that will flood through you, out into the world, and back into your life. The powerful energy of love *will* reflect love into every corner of your life!

BEING THE ENERGY FIELD OF LOVE

1. Put aware attention inward, into the center of your *being*. Feel the peace, silence, and relaxation that this focus and attention brings to you. Become aware of a light, an energy, coming from the area around your heart. A focused awareness on the light coming from your heart grows into a brilliant light.

2. Imagine yourself like a sun, a sphere of light, that is committed, giving, and nurturing, and is life itself! You have within and all around you the energy field of love. Sense, feel, or picture many lines of light representing love you have expressed and love expressed to you, going out like rays of sunlight from the area around your heart.

3. If you are ready for a new shift, affirm your readiness to awaken your heart center, making it more radiant and more magnetic. "I am ready for a new, deeper understanding of love. I surrender what I think love is and open to a new expression of love in my life."

4. Focus on the light of your heart and *be* in silence. You might imagine yourself small, surrendering as the Divine

Self magnetically draws you into the spaciousness of your heart center.

5. Your Divine Self is going ahead to do whatever is needed to awaken your heart to the next level of an expression of love that creates a more magnetic, powerful, and radiant heart center.

You have done more than you know. You have awakened your heart center that has always been there waiting for your recognition. What you contribute to the energy field of love is now more consistent and more powerful. Every thought you have that is caring, understanding, and forgiving is a connection with the energy field of love. In the same moment you think, feel, or activate an energy of loving kindness, compassion, or forgiveness a line of light goes out to the Universal Field of Love. It then gives back to you a powerful energy that you radiate out into the world and comes back again, influencing your life in good and wondrous ways.

Stop for just seconds and become aware of the powerful, infinite, and vast energy of love. It is pure goodness that strengthens and transforms. It *will* show up in your life as you become more and more aware of it. Relationships flourish and doors open wider as you feel an immersion in the infinite spaces of the energy of love. Love is pure goodness. Remember that what you think about you bring about.

As you intend and affirm a more profound expression of love than the model of love you have held, your Divine Self goes ahead to do whatever is needed to awaken your heart center. Remember that this Self is always aware of you, and truly wants to give you the best life that you are open to and ready to receive.

The energy field of love is everywhere at once. As you become more conscious of it, you can sense, feel, or simply know it is there, all around you.

In the following connection, you are expanding your magnetic heart radiance even more.

Connection in Seconds:

ALLOWING THE ENERGY OF LOVE
TO DRAW YOU INTO ITSELF

Imagine a gem of light, sparkling and lit up within the area of your heart. Sense it, feel it, fall into its beauty, its color, warmth, or perhaps, its sound. In whatever way you sense it, allow its magnetic quality to draw you into itself. As you do, your Consciousness will be transformed in this pure, clear, heartfelt light. Watch this magnetic light go out infinitely resonating with all matching energies within all lifeforms.

Connect with your radiant heart light. As you feel it, fall into it, merge with it, and know it, the more its vibrant pureness and goodness will flow into your life and the more you will know the expression of love. It reaches out further and further, matching all energies that resonate with this pure energetic light, and brings these energies back into your life.

This is the infinite Consciousness of love that flows through you, out to the world, and then back to you. You now have an awareness of the energy of love that exists all around you: a loving hug, a smile, or perhaps as you take in the beauty of nature. There are endless instances of loving gestures and kindness, which you will now be more aware of than ever.

Dr. Joe Dispenza, neuroscientist, and author, says that neuroscience can see through imaging that the brain transforms its circuitry in good, amazing ways simply as we focus on our heart.

You are becoming as radiant as the sun. It is love itself that asks for nothing in return. It is warm, nurturing, and healing.

Connection in Seconds:

CONNECTING WITH THE CLEAR, FEARLESS ENERGY OF LOVE

As you think of someone, find their clear, pure, matching energy, and connect at this level in your heart center as you embrace in the Universal energy field of love, either in your imagination or in person. Feel the matching, pure, real, and fearless love that is beyond the personality. It is Divine Consciousness that asks for nothing in return.

You may want to let several people come to mind, as you create in your mind this space of pure love.

Look for and find your expanded Consciousness of love as you go about your day. You will find that your heart center opens as you appreciate life because an attitude of appreciation and gratitude is a link to the heart. Feel, sense, link with, and know the pure goodness of the energy of love. You will find it in a loving hug, the kindness of a stranger, the excited welcoming of a pet, or as you gaze at a beautiful moonlit sky. The more you connect to it, the more you will experience it in your life and the more wondrously wonderful your life. In the following connection open to receive even more of the Consciousness of love as you send out love—a flow that gives and receives.

Connection in Seconds:

REACHING THE ENERGY OF LOVE
THROUGH CARING THOUGHTS

Keep only good, caring, understanding thoughts of others in your mind. Send lines of light like rays of sunlight out further and further, reaching the energy field of love. Watch as lines of light come back into your heart center. Allow your Divine Self to draw you into itself as you imagine yourself small, falling into your heart center. You are a vast and beautiful Consciousness of love and light.

There is a circle of love of giving and receiving. You must accept the love that you receive. This circle of love *will* come your way! The reciprocation, the giving in return, must be there because it is the natural flow of the Universe. It is a circle of love that knows no bounds and is so clear and pure nothing can touch you. It cannot be dissolved or destroyed.

As you go about your day, increase the heart connections you sense or feel by exploring, as you just did, the vast spaciousness of the heart. In this way, you are more aware of the heart connections you make with others and all life.

You have opened and awakened an awareness of the love you can give and receive more freely than ever.

Your Divine Self transforms your whole life, helping you to have a greater, consistent connection to the energy field of love. Imagine, feel, know, and embrace a focused awareness of your heart center.

AUTHOR'S MESSAGE

I congratulate you for reading this far into the book. It shows your commitment and intention to shift awareness to an easier life of less struggle and more fulfillment in every area of your life!

If you haven't already, please consider leaving a quick helpful review on Amazon.

You would be taking part in the urgent need for the evolution of human Consciousness toward a better world.

Thank you!

Darla Luz

Chapter Thirteen

LIVING DIVINE GRACE

Merging More Deeply and Peacefully with Your Divine Self

Your connection to your innermost Divine Self is more real, allowing you to understand who you truly are, your true-identity. You are also making connection in an instant, as you think of the qualities of Consciousness that are now yours, or as you picture light in the center of your being. Simply as you think of your Divine Self, you may notice a shift that tells you connection has been made. You are now more able than ever to call upon, open to, and allow a feeling of peace that is a doorway into your Divine Self.

In the following connection open to a gift of a new quality of Consciousness from your Divine Self.

Connection in Seconds:

OPENING TO A NEW QUALITY OF CONSCIOUSNESS

Rest in silent peaceful awareness, focused on your inner light. As soon as you rest in peaceful awareness, you are open and receptive. Your Divine Self knows better than you what quality would be of most benefit to you. There is nothing else to do but *be* in the effortless state of your inner Self—your Divine Self.

The light of the Divine Self flows into you, into your life, giving it a new quality. This quality of Consciousness is a gift to you that is special. You may simply sit in the light in silence knowing that the Self knows exactly what you need in every moment, or you may ask for a quality of Consciousness to add to the qualities you have gained with each connection. The qualities of inner peace, harmony and balance, and joy are just a few of many qualities that have been given to you as you have connected and opened to the higher level of Consciousness of the Self.

A new quality may feel like something you have always demonstrated. And you may not even think to link the "work" you are doing here. You are gaining qualities of Consciousness in an effortless way as you maintain connection to your innermost being—your Divine Self.

In the following practice, you are allowing your Divine Self to take hold in a more powerful way than ever.

PRACTICE #11

ALLOWING A STRONGER, FIRMER
HOLD OF YOUR DIVINE SELF

1. Feel, sense, or know the relaxation and comfort of peace.

2. In whatever way you connect, notice as you reach out to the Self, it also reaches out to you, and a shift takes place. You may or you may not feel a shift or change. Either way is fine, because this Self is always aware of you.

3. In peaceful relaxation open to this true, innermost Self, increasing its magnetic hold more firmly, to guide you, to give you its qualities that increasingly are becoming your qualities.

4. Sense the eternal, steady, and infinite nature of the Self, and realize the many qualities of Consciousness you gain as you connect. Allow, in this moment, a stronger, clearer hold of your being. Surrender and be in the light of the Self, *your* light.

5. Become aware and see clearly the changing, short-lived, unsteady aspects of the ordinary mind. Sense its dimmer light and impermanence. And become aware of the mind

of your innermost Divine Self that is permanent, stable, and strong.

6. As you become aware of the real, true, infinite light of the Divine Self, imagine turning to it as if it were a sun that is nurturing, giving, and caring. Allow this infinite light to flood your entire being, as you allow your everyday mind to turn to it as well.

7. As your mind turns toward the immense light of the Self, it is blending with its enormous light. The light flowing into the mind is radiant, real, and true, giving the mind a new quality. Watch as your everyday mind transitions into an illumined mind, so that it is no longer affected by passing, weak, impersonal thoughts.

You have done more than you know. Each connection has made it easier to call upon your Divine Self, your innermost Self and true-identity. It is there instantly as you think of it. Remember that this Self is always available and always aware of your intention to connect to it.

As the radiant light of your Divine Self fills the ordinary mind of a constantly changing, transitory nature, this mind becomes more radiant with light, so that it gradually gives the outer world of a dimmer, lesser light less importance.

As the mind transitions into brilliant light, it frees you from the worrisome, concerning aspects of an ordinary, everyday experience. The indulgence and involvement of lesser energies like sadness, anger, anxiety, and tension have fallen away. You are doing more than you know, as you flood an infinite light on the transitory, passing, and fleeting nature of the mind. As the mind becomes more radiant with light, its focus is increasingly *inward and upward*, and *not outward*, in which it focuses primarily on the outer world of problems and uncertainties, producing hardship and suffering.

It is important to remember that worrisome, concerning thoughts will reflect back into life worrisome and concerning situations and circumstances.

Remember to maintain the energies of thoughts on a higher level of Consciousness, always rising above a mood that brings you down! Turning away from negative, depressing thoughts quickly can be done by shining the powerful, radiant light of your Divine Self on your mind, as you just did.

An illumined mind is an enlightened mind. It is a mind that no longer pollutes your inner world with distress and disharmony. Remember, you still express yourself as an individual in an outer world. However, you now express an illumined mind that is an observer of an outer world and not involved in its impersonal, short-lived energies. You are driven more and more by inner peace, harmony and balance, joy, and aliveness.

If you would like to end the separation between your Divine Self and the mind, the ego, and the entire personality, give permission in the following connection.

Connection in Seconds:

SHINING DIVINE LIGHT ON
YOUR ENTIRE PERSONALITY

Imagine a luminous light coming down into the top of your head, and through your spine. It is awakening you, helping you to sustain and hold the Consciousness you have been bringing in. The entire personality is being filled with the greater illumination of your Divine Self. Simply relax, open, and be receptive in this powerfully illumined light of the Self that is merging with your entire personality, so that there is no more separation. Allow a separation to end now, in this moment. The Divine Self, mind, ego, and the personality are now one.

Your personality self is now filled with a higher level of Consciousness. New roles, new ways of being, and new understandings will appear.

The realization of who you are carries with it many gifts. And it is through surrendering that realizations and understandings come about. The realization of this Self as the truth and source of your being, also awakens Self-Realization and enlightenment.

The more you realize your oneness with your innermost Self, the more the outer world will reflect this shift and the easier it will be to create your best life. Living in the light opens you to many gifts. Little by little, problems disappear and worries dissolve. You gain perspectives, realizing that challenges are there to move life forward. As you live in the light of a higher energy, higher energies of opportunities, solutions, vitality, well-being, and more will seem like miracles. However, they are the *infinite invisible* energies that are your birthright!

As I have grown in my spiritual journey, my mind is clearer. I feel peace that is more evident than ever. A sense of well-being, aliveness, enthusiasm, and also a joy and fulfillment that comes to me effortlessly. My hope is that you are having the same realization!

Remember, once you change your Consciousness to a higher level, as you are practicing to do here, what you experience in the outer world *must* change also.

Take the illumined light that has flooded the mind of the Self, and spotlight a concerning situation, flooding it with your powerful light.

Connection in Seconds:

LETTING GO OF A CONCERNING SITUATION

Let go of any further thought about a concerning situation. Allow the light of the Self to flood the situation and let go of any desired outcome you may have. Watch as the more potent light of Divine Consciousness floods the situation. Your Consciousness is changing to a higher level—a Divine Consciousness and the situation changes *now*, instantly!

Remember that surrendering and letting go of any outcome you may want about this situation is important. Your Divine Self always knows better than you the best outcome that you need in life. Detach from the situation without giving it anymore thought. You may receive an answer now, or a solution may come in days or weeks.

A freer, more wondrous, and joyous world is opening up for you, moment to moment. You are reaching higher states and levels of Consciousness as you have connected, explored, and now express the illumined light of your Divine Self.

LIVING IN DIVINE GRACE

The light that your Divine Self has flooded into your daily life and that you are now experiencing as inner peace and new understandings is proof of your successful connection to it.

While your inner world is more peaceful and calmer, the light of your Divine Self has also manifested gifts in your outer world of joy, feelings of well-being, and a lessening of the stories and memories that have held you back.

You have now opened a path to Self-Realization and enlightenment, and you have taken a quantum leap, dramatically increasing your energetic light, your Consciousness.

In the following practice, allow a deeper closeness to this Self so that you can live more and more in the infinite invisible spaciousness of your Divine Self.

PRACTICE #12

REVEALING A NEW, MORE INFINITE WORLD OF YOUR DIVINE SELF

1. Feel the peace in this moment as you contact your Divine Self. Notice or feel the increasing light, brighter and more beautiful. Feel a deeper connection to your Divine Self as the layers of separation from the Self that have obstructed your light have fallen away.

2. Affirm your readiness to know, to come closer to your Divine Self, to become self-realized and live more and more in awareness of the infinite light and beauty of a higher world. Allow this to happen now, in this moment.

3. You have opened more into an infinite new world. Feel this lit-up world of more profound energies all around you. This is the infinite invisible of your Divine Self that will show-up in your outer as well as your inner world in daily life.

4. Surrender as never before into the brilliance of your Divine Self. Imagine yourself small, as if you are falling into an infinite Universe, immersing yourself, absorbing, and engaging with the brilliant light of the infinite invisible.

5. Open even more to this infinite invisible energy all around you. Feel it, as if you can touch it and make it more real, more solid. The brilliant light of the infinite invisible is releasing all limiting perceptions, opinions, and beliefs that have held you back, limiting you. Layer after layer of useless lesser energies are being shed, making your light more beautiful and more powerful.

6. In this moment, you are shifting your Consciousness into the Consciousness of the Divine. The "you" in daily life is becoming more expansive, unlimited, and vast. More and more of the Consciousness of the Divine is becoming yours. You have crossed the threshold into a new world.

You have done more than you know. You are releasing even more layers of limiting, restrictive views that you have held believing you were only your ordinary, everyday personality of thoughts, emotions, and body. The layers being shed are like old garments coming off, revealing a more powerful, beautiful, and brilliant inner light, and exposing even more the workings of the ordinary ego mind, giving you more clarity of thought and new understandings and realizations.

You are awakening to a greater degree the realization of your true identity, the Divine Self. You now experience the Self that knows your past, present, and future. The Self that wants to give you the best life you are open to receive. This is the Self that is now one with the ego, personality, and mind. The two selves coming together in oneness is more evident. You now realize, more than ever, the limited way in which you have lived, believing you were only the personality Self—the views, opinions, and beliefs that have kept you from creating your best life. Have great compassion for the limited self you have lived, not knowing your unlimited, infinite Divine Self that leads to an easier life of less and less struggle.

Your individuality remains in your ordinary, everyday reality, and an expression and representation of *you*, as you live in the light of the Self is more pronounced, expansive, all-encompassing, and unlimited. You now embody and express who you truly are in daily life.

The "work" you are doing as you connect and explore this Self is bringing you greater and greater rewards and gifts. As you do your part, the Divine is doing its part by going ahead and opening energy after energy, infusing you with increasingly luminous light, affecting all areas of your life.

In the following connection, give your powerful Divine Self, in full trust and surrender, permission to open the path to your highest, best future.

Connection in Seconds:

OPEN TO THE GIFT OF YOUR
HIGHEST AND BEST FUTURE

Imagine you are facing the light of your Divine Self—now your light—as if it is a sun in front of you. This is a committed, nurturing, soothing, and loving light. Allow the light to flood through you as you surrender any pictures you may have of what your future should look like. There is nothing you need to do but rest and relax in peaceful tranquility. This is a healing light that purifies and cleanses all energies that have held you back, unable to move forward in life.

Feel the relief and release you get from this connection. You have a new realization and understanding that living in the light is effortless, bringing you harmony and inner peace. Surrender what you think your future should look like in the peaceful, high vibrational energy of your Divine Self. This Self has gifts of reassurance, answers, solutions, new understandings and so much more. It can open doors to opportunities, connecting you with the right people. What comes back will be so much better than anything you could have ever imagined!

You will increasingly understand what this Self offers as you maintain a connection with it. A new outlook on life is now yours. And many gifts *will* come.

Two of my favorite gifts are the lakeview from where I write and the two books I have written. The fulfillment I feel from having written the books and the messages and reviews I have received from readers telling me I have helped them brings me much pleasure and joy!

It all began when I contemplated a lake in silence that I wrote about in the "The Heart of Attention." That experience gave me relief from the challenge I faced at the time of losing our family home. Unknowingly, I was connecting to my Divine Self in pure silence! As we connect to our true, Divine Self silently in non-thought, much more is happening and developing within than we can ever imagine!

The lakeview I once looked out at in a serene, peaceful silence, has manifested into the lakeview (not the same lake) I have today from where I write.

I want you to know that your gifts can be just as amazing, wonderful, and truly miraculous! And it all has to do with a *committed connection* to the powerful energies within each of us.

Silence is a powerful and rich space! Simply being in the rich and powerful space of silence is another way of connecting with the Divine and getting the same results. Stay connected. Imagine light—your light—because in the moment you are *aware* of your light, there is silence. The commotion and noise coming from the false mind cannot enter when you are aware in peaceful silence!

Is there a goal or a direction you want to take in which you would like guidance?

Think of an area in your life in which you would like to know the next steps to take through the guidance, inspired ideas, and direction given to you by your Divine Self.

Connection in Seconds:

INSPIRED GUIDANCE ON WHAT STEPS TO TAKE NEXT

Imagine facing the light of the Self, your Divine Self. Let go of any pictures you may have of what direction you should take. Let the light of Consciousness of the Self flood through every level of your being, inundating you with its light, allowing the flow of inspirational ideas, guidance, and insights. Surrender in trust that all is being taken care of in this moment.

Remember that your Divine Self goes ahead and opens door after door, laying out a clear path so that whatever you need— and the Divine knows exactly what you need—brings you the perfect plan, including the right people and right timing. All that you need for your higher good and best future is available and eagerly given. You are learning here to connect with the all-knowing wisdom of your Divine Self before you take action on a goal. Going into the silence of this Self and asking or simply resting in calm non-thought about what direction is best to take will lead to "knowing" and a comfortable "doing." It *does* take practice. It is the real and true *You,* discovering a space that has powerful energies to lead you effortlessly to "doing" and taking action in wise awareness, once you "know" it is right. This is the path to a more effortless life!

Feel the freedom and reassurance that you get from this connection. The flow and effortlessness when you live your true, Divine Self is real. There is no longer a need to try hard or use great effort to accomplish something you want.

There are no stressful, nerve-racking, or taxing difficulties that, in our everyday lives, are thought to be a vital part of accomplishing a goal. Living life in the light of your Divine Self becomes effortless! The "work" that needs to be done now comes from an inspirational insight or a knowing thought.

If there is an area in your life in which you have been struggling, turn to the light of your Divine Self.

Connection in Seconds:

SURRENDERING A PROBLEM OR STRUGGLE

Face your Divine self as if it is a sun that is soothing and nurturing in front of you and let go of the struggle in an area of your life. Surrender it to the light that is truth, the light that is perfect and all-knowing. Watch as the Consciousness of your Divine Self floods through you and lights up this area, dissolving it. Feel the freedom and relief as you surrender, giving you new realizations and understandings.

Only good comes from surrendering to the light of your Divine Self because you are opening in more depth to your pure, eternal, and unlimited *you*. The infinite invisible within you is opening up in a stronger way and is becoming more real, true, and solid. In the space of silent non-thought, the Self sends pure goodness into your life. One more time, face the sun of the Self in the following:

Connection in Seconds:

SURRENDERING YOUR ENTIRE
LIFE TO YOUR DIVINE SELF

Face the enormous, infinite light of the Self with the pure and open sincerity of a child. Let go of any pictures you may have of how your life should unfold. In full trust and confidence surrender your entire life to the light of the Self. Revel and bask in the powerful light, allowing it to flood your entire being and surrendering any views, thoughts, or ideas about how your life "should" turn out.

You are uncovering reliance, confidence, and trust in the Self. A Self that knows what you need in every moment beyond what you think you need. Feel the release and the relief you feel from surrendering notions, beliefs, struggles and worries.

The trust and reassurance I feel has unfolded, not only the freedom from energies that used to bring me down, but also the feelings of joy, harmony, and balance in my daily life. As I go about my day, I feel a very real joy that swells up within me for no reason at all. I may be doing a chore and I feel joy! Remember that joy does not rely on an outside world the way happiness does. "Happiness" relies on something *happening* in an outer world. Joy comes about effortlessly because the expanded space in the higher mind of the Self is pure, clear, and appreciative, free of obstructing, harmful thoughts, and emotions!

Increased supply has also become more evident. Paying down bills is now a top priority and the abundance that has unfolded in my monthly budget has been phenomenally magical. Somehow monies have come through from places I least expected. I have no doubt abundant supply is coming from the engagement with my Divine Self.

My feelings of well-being have also increased. A little over a year ago, I was diagnosed with the liver disease NAFLD and I was told that it could progress to cirrhosis and then cancer. Immediately, I changed my lifestyle to include exercise and better eating habits. I made sure my diet consisted mainly of the foods that could heal the liver, despite being told that no standard treatment exists. I quit eating processed foods and ate more organically grown food. Within a year my liver completely healed and, to my surprise, all areas of my health that were on the verge of intensifying like diabetes and inflammation were now normal, including what the doctor called a "beautiful blood pressure" reading.

I was congratulated on my healthy diagnosis with a lot of love from my family. My son congratulated my "strong will" with a bouquet of roses. The joy that surfaces in moments like these are without a doubt coming from the I AM. This is the Self, the spark that leads the way to a path awash in brilliant clarity, free of the foggy shadows of bewildered confusion that have dissolved and fallen by the wayside.

This higher level of Consciousness that showers with truly amazing gifts makes changing our entire lifestyle seem effortless.

If you feel more inner peace and calmness in your life, at this point in the book, it is an excellent start! Gifts will make their way into your life when you least expect it. You may not even connect what you have done here with improved relationships, feelings of well-being, opportunities, and greater joy.

Let go of the picture you hold in your mind of your physical body and feel your selfless, formless, invisible Self often. Feel your inner peace. These are great ways to connect!

You will realize, as I have, that it does not make sense to live a life that does not include creating and manifesting our best life!

All creation in the universe, like our creative pursuits, is the beauty and perfection that easily and effortlessly unfolds as we trust in a surrendered state.

I believe that if more of humanity lived in the light of their Consciousness—expressing the Self—we could heal not only ourselves, but our Earth and all life forms on it!

FREE MINIBOOK

To accelerate your path of letting go, feeling free, and awakening, it is important to connect *in peaceful awareness* with your true Self.

This handy **free** minibook will make it easy to connect with your true self as you go about your day. Whether you keep it next to your bedside or on your desktop, each connection will only take a few seconds of your time!

Remember that you are taking a quantum leap as you let go of daily stresses, anxieties, and past sadness to improve your situations, circumstances, and relationships!

Name _____   Email _____

Visit
www.Darlaluzbooks.com/hoaworkbook
for your free minibook

(Your free minibook will arrive in your email. Look in spam if you do not see it)

IN APPRECIATION TO ALL THE SPIRITUAL LEADERS AND AUTHORS WHO HAVE GUIDED ME ON THIS JOURNEY

To Sanaya Roman and Duane Packer for the light they have given me through their books and website, Orindaben.com. I have no doubt that Sanaya along with her gentle being of light were with me as I asked questions and quickly got answers during the writing of this book!

I encourage you to browse through the hundreds of journeys and meditations available at this website because the frequencies and vibrations received can greatly accelerate your path of self-realization and enlightenment.

To Eckart Tolle, mainly through his book "The Power of Now," that gave me a clear understanding of Consciousness.

And to authors of the following books:

Michael Singer, "The Untethered Soul"
Pema Chodron, "When Things Fall Apart"
Shakti Gawain, "Visualization"
Napoleon Hill, "Think and Grow Rich"
Esther (Abraham) Hicks, "The Law of Attraction," "Ask and It Is Given"
Rhonda Byrne, "The Secret"
Dr. Joseph Murphy, "The Power of Your Subconscious Mind"

In appreciation for the time spent listening to recordings of neuroscientist and author, Dr. Joe Dispenza, and spiritual leaders, including Deepak Chopra, Eckart Tolle, Michael Singer, Louise Hay, and Dr. Wayne Dyer.

And to the new spiritual leaders and authors who are opening the door wider for humanity to enter and know who they truly are.

CAN YOU HELP?

Please take a moment to leave a helpful review on
Amazon. I read all reviews and would greatly appreciate
yours. You would be helping to reach thousands around the
globe to live a better, more joyous life, free of inner turmoil.

With your helpful review, you would be
taking part in the urgent need for the evolution of
human Consciousness for a better world.

Thank you!

Darla Luz

ABOUT THE AUTHOR

Darla Luz is an award-winning writer who is passionate about expanding and evolving Consciousness throughout the world by writing about it in an easy to understand way. She lives what she has written in this book, knowing that our outer world always reflects the pure positivity of our inner world. Most days are spent doing her life's work of practicing her own expansion of Consciousness, and researching and writing about it so that she can help others be consciously aware in presence, free of struggle and inner turmoil. She enjoys taking nature walks with her family observing the natural wilderness along the riverbanks and lakesides near her home.

www.ingramcontent.com/pod-product-compliance
Lightning Source LLC
Chambersburg PA
CBHW031547040426
42452CB00006B/218